Daisy Pulls It Off

A Comedy

Denise Deegan

Samuel French - London
New York - Toronto - Hollywood

DAISY PULLS IT OFF

First performed at the Nuffield Theatre, Southampton, on 13th January, 1983, with the following cast of characters:

Daisy Meredith	Alexandra Mathie
Mother	Caroline Goodall
Monica Smithers	Adrienne Thomas
Clare Beaumont	Kate Buffery
Sybil Burlington	Edita Brychta
Alice Fitzpatrick	Samantha Bond
Trixie Martin	Helena Little
Miss Gibson	Charlotte West-Oram
Headmistress	Charlotte West-Oram
Miss Granville	Rosalind Adler
Mademoiselle	Caroline Goodall
Belinda Mathieson	Sarah Harper
Winnie Irving	Rosalind Adler
Dora Johnston	Caroline Goodall
Mr Scoblowski	Roger Heathcott
Mr Thompson	Alex Johnston
Drunken Man	Alex Johnston
School Pianist	Renie Wright

The play directed by David Gilmore
Designed by Glenn Willoughby
Lighting designed by Brian Harris

The action of the play takes place in and around the environs of Grangewood School for Girls

Period: 1927

Subsequently presented by Andrew Lloyd Webber at the Globe Theatre, London, on 18th April, 1983, with the following cast of characters.

Daisy Meredith	Alexandra Mathie
Mother	Carol Ann Crawford
Monica Smithers	Adrienne Thomas
Clare Beaumont	Kate Buffery
Sybil Burlington	Edita Brychta
Alice Fitzpatrick	Sarah Mortimer
Trixie Martin	Helena Little
Miss Gibson	Charlotte West-Oram
Miss Granville	Rosalind Adler
Mademoiselle	Carol Ann Crawford
Belinda Mathieson	Sarah Harper
Winnie Irving	Rosalind Adler
Dora Johnston	Carol Ann Crawford
Mr Scoblowski	Roger Heathcott
Mr Thompson	Philip Guard
School Pianist	Liz Buffery
Staff and Girls	Lisa Anselmi, Ruth Kenley, Robin Miller, May Spence, Rodney Wood

The play directed by David Gilmore
Designed by Glenn Willoughby
Lighting designed by Brian Harris

PRODUCTION NOTE

This Acting Edition is based on the production seen at the Globe Theatre, London, wherein several techniques were employed, including revolves, which may not be available for subsequent productions.

The settings moved swiftly from, for example, a train to the school, from the library to the dormitory and so on, several levels being used as well as the revolves. However, staging can be simplified as long as smoothness and speed are aimed for, without complicated scenery changes. As explained below, the narrative dialogue of the characters can be used to cover any setting of props etc., which should be kept to a minimum—just suggesting the setting.

The dialogue of the majority of characters fulfils two purposes. Speech may be directed to the audience (as an "aside" so to speak) when that character is introducing itself or continuing the narrative of the story. Speech will also be directed to the other persons of the play, as would normally be expected. These two types of dialogue are clearly marked as:

(*to the audience*) or (*narrating*)—when introducing themselves, or continuing narrative

(*to*, for example, *Trixie*)—when speaking to characters on stage

The music for the School Song (p. 51) is available on free loan from Samuel French Ltd

The photographs in this Acting Edition are by Paul Carter of Viewpoint, Southampton

ACT I

Grangewood School for Girls

Miss Gibson the Head-mistress, the Staff and Pupils welcome the audience to the school as they enter the auditorium. Moving among the audience with such words as "Hello to you", "So glad you could make sports day", "Ah! an old girl" etc. A teacher plays suitable tunes on the piano. When everyone is in, Miss Gibson stands CS *with the staff and pupils in a semi-circle around her*

Miss Gibson (*to the audience*) Good evening. May I, before we begin the evening's entertainment, take this opportunity to welcome you—parents, brothers, sisters, cousins, uncles, aunts, friends and, for aught I know, grandparents too—to Grangewood School for Girls. Today marks the twenty-fifth anniversary of the founding of the school, twenty-five years of consistent sporting and academic achievement, of targets striven towards and goals attained, of aspiration and realization, from which has evolved amongst pupils and staff, a tradition of fairness to one's fellow creatures, loyalty to school and country, a sense of duty and honour, of being straight and playing the game, and above all, a tradition of happy girls. May that tradition still be cleaven to on the fiftieth anniversary of this establishment.
Voice Off Hear, hear.
Miss Gibson I won't detain you any longer except to explain that each form in the school has assumed responsibility for one entire evening's entertainment during the course of this festival week. The mantle of responsibility falls tonight, by lottery, on the Fourth form, together with a little help from members of staff, who have asked me to announce their offering, a play in two acts entitled *Daisy Pulls It Off*. Thank you.

Everyone exits except Daisy who puts on a dressing-gown and stands CS

Daisy (*to the audience*) Daisy Meredith, daredevil, tomboy, possessed of a brilliant mind, exuberant, quick-witted, fond of practical jokes, honourable, honest, courageous, straight in all things and ... an elementary school pupil. Father—dead. Mother—a former opera singer who struggles to keep a home together for herself, Daisy, and Daisy's brothers—Dick, Douglas, Daniel and Duncan in a small terraced house in London's East End, by giving music lessons to private pupils. Daisy has recently taken an exam which will, if she succeeds in passing it, enable her to gain a place as the first ever scholarship pupil at Grangewood Girls School, one of the most famous educational establishments in the country. If, however, she fails the exam, she must leave her elementary school at the end of the year and take up some form of ill-paid menial work to which she is little suited. Thank you. (*To herself*) I do wish the postman would hurry and bring the letter containing the exam results—but it isn't even eight o'clock yet. I must win the scholarship, I so want to go to Grangewood. How topping it would be to learn Latin and Greek, to play hockey on their famous pitch, to make friends with all those jolly girls and have midnight feasts and get into fearful scrapes just like they do in books. I should miss mother and Dick, Douglas, Daniel and Duncan of course . . . and all my chums at elementary school. But I must win the scholarship for the sake of others as well as for myself, for if I, the first scholarship pupil at Grangewood, make a success of the scheme, Grangewood will open its doors to other elementary school pupils, as poor as myself.

Sybil Burlington enters

Sybil So, elementary schoolgirls at Grangewood; bringing their dishonesty, filth and guttersnipe ways with them and generally lowering the tone of the place. Well, we'll see about that. (*She starts to exit—then stops and turns. To the audience*) Oh, Sybil Burlington, Vice-Captain of the Upper Fourth, and conceited, beautiful, only daughter of very wealthy parents.

Sybil exits

Daisy Mother! Oh, Mother, I'm through! I've got the scholarship! I can go to Grangewood!

Mother enters and during the following helps Daisy get into the rest of her school uniform

Mother Daisy, dear, that's splendid, I'm so glad and proud.

Daisy I hope I make a success of it.

Mother You will, my dear, you've got this far.

Daisy I'll have a good education, pass all my exams and then, when I leave, find a job as a teacher in an elementary school and perhaps I'll earn enough money to buy you the country cottage you've always wanted, and to pay for Dick, Douglas, Daniel and Duncan's education if they haven't won scholarships by then. (*To the audience*) The summer holidays passed all too slowly for Daisy, that is, until the time came to say goodbye to those she loved best.

Mother Board the train, Daisy, dear, otherwise you'll find yourself on the platform and the train steaming off without you. Oh, the boys asked me to give you this. (*She hands Daisy a small package*)

Daisy Write often, Mother, I'll be dying to know what you're all doing, and any news you may hear of my old school pals.

Mother God bless you, Daisy, dear, I know you'll do absolutely splendidly and make us all even prouder of you, if that's possible. And remember, Daisy, keep your chin up, and never tell a lie or do anything mean or underhand. You might find boarding school life strange or perhaps difficult at first, but be straight with everyone and you'll pull through.

A whistle blows, off

Daisy We're off—oh, Mother—

Mother and Daisy hug and kiss

Mother Good-bye, my darling—write soon . . .
Daisy See you at the end of term!

Mother exits

Sybil Burlington and Belinda Mathieson enter

Sybil (*to the audience*) Meanwhile, in the adjoining carriage . : .
Belinda (*to the audience*) Belinda Mathieson, Captain of the Upper Fourth
and best all round sportswoman of that form. (*To Sybil*) What utter rot
you talk, Sybil, not all elementary school kids live in filthy hovels with
thieving fathers and drunken sluttish mothers. Take a walk through Esher
any day. And if this . . . Daisy Meredith is brainy enough to win a
scholarship to Grangewood, she's as much right to a good education as
the rest of us there.
Sybil But don't you see, Belinda, that if this Meredith girl proves a success
then Grangewood will lose the type of person that's made it into the kind
of school it is today. I heard several girls—and teachers—last term saying
how unhappy they were about the scheme.
Belinda Even Miss Gibson?
Sybil Miss Gibson will soon see sense when exam standards drop and girls
leave and Grangewood loses every sports trophy it's ever won. Hockey
and tennis aren't taught in elementary schools.
Belinda How frightful.
Daisy (*to the audience*) The journey passed miserably for Daisy until the
train made a stop at a small country station.

Clare Beaumont enters

Clare (*to the audience*) Clare Beaumont, Head Girl and Sports Captain of
Grangewood School, a shining example of true British girlhood. (*To
Daisy*) Excuse me, are any of these seats taken?
Daisy Just mine.
Clare Bound for Grangewood School, I see.
Daisy Yes.
Clare I don't recall having seen you before.
Daisy No, it's my first term, actually.
Clare Well, I'm sure you'll be tremendously happy with us, Grangewood is
the jolliest school in England. Clare Beaumont, by the way, sixth.
Daisy Daisy Meredith.
Clare Daisy Meredith . . .
Daisy Yes, I'm to be in the Upper Fourth.
Clare Of course, you must be the girl who won the scholarship.
Daisy The first of many such girls, I hope.
Clare That's the spirit, kiddie, but there are a few silly little rotters in the
school who aren't too keen on scholarship pupils being admitted. I'd lie

low if I were you, for the first month or so until they've got used to the
idea being made flesh. Buck-up, child, there are some quite decent girls in
the Fourth, you'll pull through.

Daisy I jolly well hope to.

Clare Here we are at the station.

Alice (*off*) Clare! Clare, old girl!

Clare Coming! The school is only five minutes away, you'll find it easily
enough, just follow the others. Chin-up, kiddie . . .

Alice (*off*) Clare!

Clare See you later, I expect.

*All the girls and mistresses enter with luggage, acting out Daisy's words as
she speaks*

Daisy (*to the audience*) Daisy stepped on to the platform of the tiny country
station, scarcely able to push her way through the crowd of laughing,
chattering girls—girls of all shapes and sizes—girls merrily exchanging
greetings and holiday reminiscences with chums whom they had not seen
for seven long weeks—girls who in the blue and white colours of
Grangewood School resembled not so much a whirlpool, as so many
tumbling, foaming little waves rushing shorewards on the incoming tide
and breaking thankfully on the warm, yellow sands of home. Mistresses
suddenly appeared on the platform and began to shepherd the bubbling
throng into the lane that led to the school. They rounded the corner—I
say!—and there stood Grangewood School, a rambling red-brick Eliza-
bethan mansion, its mullioned windows twinkling in the sun like so many
welcoming eyes beneath curious twisted chimneys. Flowers of every scent
and hue bordered the smooth green lawns, and there behind the house
stretched the tennis courts and playing fields for which Grangewood was
justly renowned. As they passed through the great stone gates, the girls—
as one—turned to look at the sapphire sea beating against the chalky
cliffs on which the school so proudly stood. What an absolutely gorgeous
place, I'm going to be so immensely happy here.

Trixie Isn't it heavenly?

Daisy I'm knocked over entirely.

Trixie (*to the audience*) Trixie Martin, madcap and poet of the Upper
Fourth. (*To Daisy*) I say aren't you a new bug . . . I mean girl.

Daisy Yes, Daisy Meredith.

Trixie Daisy Meredith?

Daisy That's right, I'm to be in the Upper Fourth.

Trixie O Jubilate, that's my form. Perhaps we can have desks next to each
other. One can have an uncommonly good time at Grangewood so long
as one doesn't upset the prees or mistresses too much. I say, are you fond
of setting up stunts?

Daisy I should say. I've got four brothers and we constantly play tricks on
each other.

Trixie Can you swim?

Daisy A little.

Trixie Capital, you'll soon improve, for if the weather's fine enough the entire school goes for an early morning dip in the sea. There's an absolutely scrummy beach at the bottom of the cliffs with a secret path leading down to it known only to ourselves.

Daisy How perfectly ripping.

Clare and Alice enter

Trixie That's Claire Beaumont, over there, she's—

Daisy I've met her.

Trixie How uncommonly lucky. Clare is Grangewood's Sports Captain and Head Girl, she's a first-rate tennis and hockey player as well as having a brain. We all adore her. Her people, well, her mother, actually own Grangewood ...

Daisy I say!

Trixie ... her family used to live in the building and then just over twenty years ago, they started to lose money after old Sir Digby Beaumont died and so they leased it out to the school govenors. Each year the Beaumonts have lost more and more money and now it looks as though they might have to sell to the School Governors. There is talk that the family fortunes could be saved if only the Beaumont treasure could be found!

Daisy Treasure!

Trixie Yes! I've hunted for hours tapping walls, looking for secret panels and trapdoors and clues, and so have scores of other girls, but it's probably only hearsay, nothing's ever been found.

Monica Smithers enters

Monica Trixie Martin, you're to go and see Matron at once, she's in a fearful mood over something.

Trixie Oh dash it! Mother's probably not name-tagged my new socks. See you at tea, I expect, Daisy.

Trixie exits

Monica (*to the audience*) Monica Smithers, school toady and chief crony of Sybil Burlington. (*To Daisy*) I say, I've not seen you before.

Daisy It's my first day at Grangewood—Daisy Meredith.

Monica Daisy ... oh, the scholarship girl.

Daisy That's right.

Monica Ever been to school before?

Daisy Yes, of ...

Monica Read and write, can you?

Daisy What on ...

Monica Elementary schoolgirls are a new breed at Grangewood, you see, we've no idea what to expect. Not that I've ever been in a position to meet anyone from an elementary school before, Mummy and Daddy are so frightfully particular about that kind of thing. Of course, in our situation one has to be, some people will do anything for money. Oh, by the way, Miss Gibson always likes to see new girls in her study on their first day.

Daisy Really?

Monica Up this staircase, first door on the right.

Daisy Thank you.

Monica exits

What a sickening girl! Now where did she say, up the staircase, and the
first door on the right. Now to meet the Head.

Daisy knocks on the door—no answer. She knocks again—still no answer

Alice Fitzpatrick enters

Alice (*to the audience*) Alice Fitzpatrick, Prefect, Deputy Sports Captain
and best chum of Clare Beaumont. (*To Daisy*) And what are you
knocking on there for, child?

Daisy I've got to see Miss Gibson.

Alice Well, it's not in there you'll find Miss Gibson, see, 'tis only a broom
cupboard.

Daisy Oh, but I was told . . .

Alice Someone playing a trick on you, was it? I'll take you meself to Miss
Gibson. You're a new girl by the look of things.

Daisy Yes, I am. My name's Daisy Meredith and I'm to be in the Upper
Fourth.

Alice Daisy . . . well that's a nice enough name. Are you fond of games,
hockey, tennis and suchlike?

Daisy I enjoy playing cricket and football with my brothers, but I've not
had much opportunity to play hockey or tennis, you see they didn't teach
them at my last school. Only rounders.

Alice Is that a fact?

Daisy But I know all the rules for hockey and tennis, I swotted up on them
from books at home.

Alice Reading's not quite the same as doing, but if you have the sporting
spirit you'll do finely. Play the game, that's what we say here, play up and
play the game—and it's a poor view we take of any girl who doesn't play
it.

Daisy (*indicating a wooden board*) What's that?

Alice The School Honours Board. A record of achievements by girls whom
Grangewood is truly proud to have had within its portals.

Daisy (*narrating*) Daisy gazed wistfully at the simple oak boards with the
names graven in gold of former pupils. I mean Grangewood to be proud
of me one day and perhaps my name to shine amongst theirs.

Alice Here we are, child, Miss Gibson's room.

Daisy Fearfully kind of you to help me.

Alice All my pleasure, child. Run along in, Miss Gibson will not bite your
head off.

Alice exits

Miss Gibson enters

Miss Gibson (*to the audience*) Miss Gibson, young, much-loved, headmistress of Grangewood School.

Daisy Daisy Meredith, ma'am.

Miss Gibson Welcome, my dear, to Grangewood, how very pleased we are to have you here.

Daisy Thank you.

Miss Gibson I need not say, of course, that the advent of Grangewood's first scholarship pupil—one who has arrived here by way of intellect and not by way of parental monetary wealth—has caused a certain amount of trepidation within the school. Much will be expected of you, both morally and intellectually, but from the scholastic reports I have received of you and from the impressions I have of the girl standing here before me, I am sure that you will fulfil all expectations. Everyone will be anxious to help you in any way you may require during your first few weeks here—as we do all new girls. I hope you will be very happy here, my dear, and will always stay true to the motto of Grangewood, which is also that of the Beaumont family whose ancestral home this is—*Honesta quam magna*—How great are noble things. Now I'm sure you're tired, Daisy, the supper bell will be ringing shortly and Matron will wish to see you before then. I trust you will settle in quickly, my child. Well, run along.

Daisy Thank you, Miss Gibson.

Miss Gibson exits

Phew.

Trixie enters

Trixie Hello. I say, isn't it capital, you're to be in the same dormy as me!

Daisy How glorious!

Trixie Dormy number five, one of the best, it looks out over the sea . . .

Daisy How topping.

Trixie Worst luck is, we've to share it with that stuck-up pair of prigs, Sybil Burlington and Monica Smithers. I expect Miss Gibson thinks they'll set us a good example. Miss Gibson is an uncommonly jolly headmistress, but I feel she can be immensely misguided sometimes. Still, Jean Jeffrey and Dora Johnston are next door in number three so we can organize a stunt or two between the four of us.

Daisy Midnight feasts.

Trixie A chum after my own heart. I say, what's that? (*She indicates the package given to Daisy earlier by her mother*)

Daisy A farewell present from my four brothers. I shall miss them tremendously, I've never been away from home before.

Trixie Grangewood's a decent place, you'll survive.

Daisy It's queer, Trixie, but I already feel strangely at home in Grangewood, almost as if I'd been here before.

A bell rings, off

Trixie O Jubilate, there goes the supper bell. Come on, we can sit wherever we like first day back.

Trixie exits

Daisy (*to the audience*) After supper, a substantial if plain meal, during

which due to the jolly conversation of her friend, Daisy failed to notice
the somewhat disdainful and curious glances cast at her by several of her
fellow pupils, Daisy decided to take a stroll into the great hall to study the
ancestral portraits of the Beaumont family which hung there. Oh! (*she
opens the package*) A frog! I know!

*Daisy exits one side of the stage (to the dormitory), re-enters minus the
small brown package, then exits the other side*

*Trixie then enters and goes through the dormitory door then re-enters and
exits giggling*

Sybil and Monica enter, in dressing-gowns

Sybil Honestly, Monica, it's the absolute limit, not only do we have to
suffer this girl in the same form room, but we have to share the hitherto
unpolluted air of our dormy with her as well. Not to mention that
tiresome little wretch, Trixie Martin. And it's one of the nicest dormys in
the school.

Monica Have you noticed, Sybil, how extraordinarily chummy Trixie is
with the Meredith girl?

Sybil Yes, we must put a stop to that. For the sake of Grangewood.

Sybil }
Monica } (*together*) *Honesta quam Magna.*

Trixie enters

Trixie Hello, Sybil, Monica. Daisy here?

Sybil Whom?

Trixie You know Daisy Meredith, she's in our dormy.

Sybil The scholarship girl?

Trixie That's right, Daisy Meredith.

Sybil Trixie, if you really care for Grangewood and wish to maintain its
tone and its reputation on the playing field, not forgetting the good name
of the Upper Fourth, you will cease your friendship with Daisy Meredith.

Trixie Why?

Sybil Scholarship girls are different from us, they're poor, perhaps not
intellectually, but certainly morally.

Trixie Perhaps they should be given a chance to rise from their poorness.

Sybil And what will happen to us, to Grangewood, to England, the
Empire? We have to accept, Trixie, that different classes of people exist in
this world.

Trixie You're an unspeakable snob, Sybil. I heard all about the meeting
you held in the common-room, give Daisy a perfectly ghastly time of it so
she'll want to leave Grangewood. Well I, for one, won't have anything to
do with such a thoroughly horrid scheme. Daisy's a capital girl, she got
here through brains not money, and I mean to stick by her.

Trixie exits

Sybil Silly little rotter.

Monica Well, I think you're right, Sybil.

Sybil Thank you, Monica, it's a sad thing when there are only two people in an entire school who really care about it. I'll take my cocoa to bed, I think.

Monica And me.

Sybil and Monica exit to the dormitory

Screams are heard off. Seconds later Sybil enters holding a rubber frog, with Monica holding a hairbrush. Trixie and Daisy enter at the same time

Sybil Who, may I ask, put these in our beds?

Daisy |
Trixie | *(together)* Your beds?

Sybil Yes.

Daisy I'm afraid it was I who put the frog into your bed, I'm fearfully sorry, you see I thought it was Trixie's bed and the frog a present from . . .

Sybil Just the sort of behaviour one expects from . . .

Trixie And I put the hairbrush into your bed, Monica, thinking that it was Daisy's.

Monica |
Sybil | *(together)* Typical.

Trixie Only ragging, nothing to pour the vials of wrath about. Daisy, our two dormy mates, Sybil Burlington and Monica Smithers.

Daisy Hello.

Trixie Monica, Sybil, allow me to introduce Daisy Meredith, newest ornament of the Upper Fourth.

Monica |
Sybil | *(together)* H'm!

Trixie Scooterons-nous, Daisy? We won't get our cocoa otherwise.

Trixie exits

Daisy Yes. Jolly nice to have met you both.

Monica and Sybil exit

(*Narrating*) After a delightful early morning dip in the sparkling sea, a short prayer service and a jolly breakfast, or brekker as it was known amongst the girls, Daisy, with the rest of her form, trooped into the Upper Fourth class-room, there to commence her first lesson, English composition.

Daisy exits

The pupils, including Sybil and Monica, enter the class-room

Sybil and Monica, unseen by the others, smear chalk on Daisy's desk seat and put a comic under her desk lid

Miss Granville enters

Miss Granville (*to the audience*) Miss Granville, the firm but fair form-mistress of the Upper Fourth, one of the teachers with strong doubts on the efficacy of scholarship pupils at Grangewood. (*To the pupils*) Good morning, girls.

Girls Good morning, Miss Granville.

Miss Granville Now girls, open your poetry books please, at page number fifty-five. We are going to read "Ye Mariners of England" a Naval Ode by Thomas Campbell. Daisy, Daisy Meredith, can we hear you read this please. Stand out here.

The Girls giggle as Daisy comes out with the chalk smeared on the back of her gymslip

Daisy   Ye Mariners of England
                     That guard our native seas!
                     Whose flag has braved a thousand years
                     The battle and the breeze!
                     Your glorious standard launch again
                     To meet another foe;
                     And sweep through the deep,
                     While the stormy tempests blow!
                     While the battle rages loud and long
                     And the stormy winds do blow.

Miss Granville Girls, please, I will not have this giggling during my lesson. The holidays finished yesterday, you are here to work. Thank you, Daisy, an excellent reading, you may return to your seat. Belinda, will you ... Daisy, come here please. What is that on the back of your gymslip? You have a white patch on the back of your gymslip.

Daisy It's chalk, Miss Granville.

Miss Granville Brush it off then. Why on earth you are covered with chalk I cannot imagine. Please remember, Daisy, you are not in elementary school now, we like Grangewood girls to look presentable not as though they have been tobogganing down the sides of chalk pits. You may return to your place. Monica, have you anything to say to me? Then kindly refrain from gossiping to your neighbours. I have a brief appointment to keep with Miss Gibson, so I will leave you to study the poem alone, and also the poems on pages fifty-four, fifty-seven and fifty-eight. For your composition after you've read the poems, I want you to choose one of the following exercises, Pens ready? One. Is Patriotism productive of poetry? If so, why? Two. Summarize in headings the causes of England's greatness. Three. What difference would it make to the world if the British Isles were submerged by the sea? Daisy, what do I see protruding from beneath your desk lid? A comic.

Daisy But it isn't ...

Miss Granville I shall confiscate this. Comics—dreadful rags—are confined to the common room. I would usually give an order mark for such an offence, but as you are new I shall let you off. There is a copy of the school rules on the notice board. I suggest you make a point of reading them. Girls, I shall see you shortly. Belinda, take charge please.

Belinda Yes, Miss Granville.

Miss Granville exits

Daisy I'd like to thank whoever was responsible for nearly getting me an order mark.

Monica Shhhhh.

Trixie First time you've ever kept silent without a mistress in the room, Monica.

Monica Tit for tat.

Trixie Stunts are fine, Sybil, as long as one doesn't land one's victim in a hole. Order marks aren't my idea of fun.

Sybil Is your friend incapable of speaking up for herself?

Daisy No, just speechless at some people's meanness.

Belinda As Captain of the form, I ask you to kindly chuck all this talking and get down to some work before a mistress comes along and hears us.

Silence. Then from outside comes the sound of someone whistling the tune "All Through the Night". Daisy looks up as though the tune touches an old memory that she can't recall

Daisy Belinda, who is that whistling outside?

Belinda Mr Thompson. He's employed here as an assistant gardener. Rather a mystery man, he lives alone in a tiny cottage in the middle of Cramphorn Wood. Where he comes from no-one knows. He suddenly appeared in the area about ten years ago, apparently. He hasn't a wife or any relatives that visit him or anything of that sort.

Daisy Poor man.

Monica I say, Sybil, isn't Meredith a name of Welsh origin?

Sybil I do believe it is, Monica.

Monica My father tells me that the Welsh keep their house coals in their baths. How quaint.

Daisy Why are you being so beastly to me, both of you? You've paid me back for the frog-in-the-bed stunt.

Sybil Are elementary school-kids incapable of taking a joke?

Belinda Chuck it, Sybil, you really are being pretty hateful. This is Daisy's first morning here, we should be showing her what Grangewood girls are made of, not acting like a pack of mean cats. And I, for one, won't stand to hear her called an elementary school-kid, she's a Grangewood girl now, one of us, scholarship or not.

Sybil You needn't be so beastly pi, Belinda . . .

Belinda I refuse to discuss the matter further.

Sybil Very well, Belinda, you form your own little gallery of plaster saints, but you'll soon see whether I'm right or not, all of you.

A bell rings off

Mr Scoblowski enters

The Girls stand up

Mr Scoblowski (*to the audience*) Mr Scoblowski, the enigmatic, Russian, music-teacher. Good morning, girls.

Girls Good morning, Mr Scoblowski.

Mr Scoblowski Remain standing. Now to begin we will all sing the song *The Ash Grove.*

The Girls sing the song. Mr Scoblowski walks among them listening to their voices

H'mm. We have much work to do if you are to present yourselves well at the end of term concert. You sing straight from the throat not enough from here, you strain the voice otherwise. However, there is one excellent voice among you. (*He indicates Daisy*) It is this young lady who sings so sublimely. Sing the next verse alone if you please.

Daisy sings the verse

Excellent, excellent. Did you mark how she controlled her voice and her breathing. What is your name? You are a new girl.

Daisy Daisy Meredith.

Mr Scoblowski Ah, Meredith, a Welsh name. You have a voice truly representative of that musical nation. I shall see that you have a solo in the end of term concert. Excellent voice, excellent. And you, Miss Burlington, will have to prove to me that you are not as tone-deaf as you seem to be, if you wish also to take your place in the choir. Now we will sing the song *Cherry Ripe.*

They sing the song

After the song everyone exits except Daisy and Trixie who fling themselves to the ground

Daisy I say, my head's absolutely spinning.

Trixie You're doing uncommonly well, Daisy, everyone's tremendously impressed.

Daisy All except Monica and Sybil.

Trixie They're thoroughly piggy and nasty, don't let's waste our dinner break over them. You speak French like a native, I didn't think they taught it in elementary schools.

Daisy They don't, my mother taught me.

Trixie My word!

Daisy And Italian, all my brothers speak it too. You see, she used to be an opera singer.

Trixie A singer?

Daisy I'm afraid so.

Trixie Oh no, I find it tremendously exciting.

Pause

Daisy I say, Trixie . . . let's form a Secret Society.

Trixie A Secret Society?

Daisy Yes, just like they do in schools in books. I know, a treasure-hunting society, its object to seek out the treasure of Grangewood School and so rescue the Beaumonts from penury. We could ask some of the others if they'd like to become members.

Trixie They won't and anyway everyone else has stopped believing that the treasure exists. As a rule one ceases to believe in it by the time one reaches the Lower Third, rather like fairies and Father Christmas. Everyone that is except poetical types such as myself, romantically minded new girls and possibly Clare. No, let it just be the two of us.

Daisy And let's call ourselves, I know, the Dark Horse Secret Society.

Trixie Oh yes . . .!

Daisy It can be our secret symbol whenever we have to write each other notes.

Trixie Oh heavenly! We must have a motto too, a password. Um . . . *audacia et virtute adepta* . . . too long! *Absque virtute nihil* . . . no! Ah, how about this, *hinc spes effulget!*

Daisy Yes. Sorry, I've no idea what it means, I've no Latin.

Trixie Hence hope shines forth!

Daisy Oh topping, Trixie! Hence hope shines forth.

A bell rings off

Trixie We'd better dash, there goes the bell for afternoon games. Hockey for the fourth.

Daisy I expect I shall get horribly beaten, I've never played hockey before.

Trixie Hockey is a team game, you play as a team and win or lose as one, remember that.

Daisy I will.

Daisy and Trixie exit
Clare and Alice enter with hockey sticks

Alice Isn't it a fine thing to be back in the old school, to be standing on this pitch where we've fought so many battles.

Clare Yes, Alice, it is as you say, a fine thing. You know, I'm almost glad this is my final year at Grangewood, for it may be the last year that the name of Beaumont will appear upon the title deeds.

Alice Dear girl!

Clare The truth of the matter is, Alice, we're up a gum tree. What with poor mother's medical fees and my younger brother—

Alice Digby?

Clare Yes, dear Digby's school fees have still to be met, and the rent of the cottage is far too high for us. I was talking with mother before I came back. Unless a miracle happens, we'll have to sell to the School Governors by Christmas. I offered to leave school and find employment as a teacher, but mother wouldn't hear of it. I must say, I'm not looking forward to leaving all this, going out into the world and becoming a proper grown-up. They say Grangewood is supposed to mirror the world. I wonder . . . My goodness, someone's playing a first rate game of hockey over here.

Alice It's the Upper Fourth . . . a practice game by the looks of things. Who's that child there? She can certainly pass balls.

Clare It's the new kiddie, the scholarship girl, Daisy Meredith. With some proper coaching she could be a decent player. Look at her, never funking a single ball.

Alice Learnt all the rules from a book, I was told.

Clare A sportsman as well as a scholar.

Alice There's one whose name will grace the First Eleven.

Clare Well, old girl, let's go off to our own practice, we've a match to win on Saturday, the opening knock-out game of the County Championships. Perhaps this year we'll come out tops.

Alice Instead of runners-up as we have been for the past ten years to Vearncombe Young Ladies College.

Voice (*off*) Clare! Alice!

Clare There's Diana calling us. As the middles say—scooterons-nous, Alice.

Clare exits

Alice We'll beat them this year, for Grangewood ... for Clare. We must.

Alice exits

Daisy and Trixie enter

Daisy (*narrating*) For a while, Daisy's life at Grangewood passed uneventfully, apart from the odd unpleasantness from Sybil and Monica. Then one evening after prep while she and Trixie were systematically tapping wooden wall panels in the hope of finding a secret passage which would lead them to the hidden treasure ...

Mr Scoblowski enters

Mr Scoblowski What are you girls doing here? Don't you know that this gallery is out of bounds to all but teachers and prefects.

Trixie Yes, Sir.

Mr Scoblowski Then kindly tell me the reason why you are here or I shall report you to your form mistress.

Pause

If you choose not to tell me, you will have to tell Miss Granville. And perhaps receive an order mark.

Daisy We were looking for the treasure, sir ...

Mr Scoblowski Treasure?

Daisy The lost treasure of the Beaumont family.

Mr Scoblowski Ah, I see. Well, you will not find it here. I myself, have often sought its whereabouts and have carefully examined this entire section of the building, and now I believe this treasure to be a legend, a mere myth. However, should you come across any clue elsewhere in the school, I should be most happy to know of it. I am much fascinated by the folk-tales of the English. Good night, ladies.

Mr Scoblowski exits

Trixie Why the dickens did you tell him what we were doing, Daisy?

Daisy We would have had to have told Miss Granville, otherwise, who would certainly have given us an order mark for going out of bounds.

Trixie Oh, what a dismal beastly sell, it's obvious Mr Scoblowski's after the treasure for himself.

Daisy Probably to try and help his Bolshevik friends.

Trixie We simply must try out the rest of this gallery. But how?

Daisy I know, how about sneaking out of the dormy at dead of night.

Trixie Oh, yes.

Daisy Perhaps we could borrow a couple of cloaks from Matron and disguise ourselves as ghostly monks to scare off anyone who might see us.

Trixie Capital suggestion.

A bell rings off

Supper bell.

Daisy Not a word to anyone, Trixie.

Trixie Until I wake you.

Trixie ⎱
Daisy ⎰ *(together) Hinc spes effulget.*

They both shake hands—a special handshake—then exit

Monica and Sybil enter in dressing-gowns

Sybil The scheme isn't working out, Monica.

Monica It is in small ways, Sybil.

Sybil So small that it's going to take twenty years for her to collect enough order marks to get a bad conduct mark. No, Monica, she's doing fearfully well in everyone's books, we've got to move drastically ... and fast.

Whistling is heard, off—"All Through the Night". Monica listens to it intently

Look, Monica, do you like this solid silver bracelet Daddy sent me as a pre-birthday present? I say, Monica, do look ...

Monica Oh, sorry Sybil.

Sybil I've permission from Miss Gibson for Daddy to take me out to a slap-up birthday tea in town and then off to a concert afterwards and Daddy said I might invite a friend to accompany me. I'm thinking of asking you, Monica.

Monica Oh, Sybil, I'd adore it.

Sybil All serene then. Now I'm going to read some Keats in preparation for the school poetry competition. I mean to win it this year, not to be pipped at the post by that wretched Trixie Martin.

Monica When do entries have to be in?

Sybil Oh, in three to four weeks I believe. Why, Monica, are you thinking of entering?

Monica Yes ... oh ... I mean, I could never hope to write anything that would be half as good as anything of yours, Sybil, but I do have a tremendous fancy to have a bash at it. Just to show that Daisy Meredith a thing or two.

Sybil Well, bash away to your heart's content ... I'm off to bed.

Sybil and Monica exit

A clock strikes two—night

Trixie and Daisy enter in long black cloaks with hoods. Daisy trips noisily

Daisy Ooh!
Trixie Shhh!
Daisy I say, Trixie, it's fearfully dark.
Trixie I've brought a torch.
Daisy Oh, scrummy. I say, did you hear Sybil snoring?

They both giggle

Trixie Come on—to the gallery. Now we must be very quiet.

Daisy and Trixie creep up the stairs

Sybil enters. She creeps stealthily across the stage and exits

Trixie We're almost there. I say, what's that?
Daisy What?
Trixie Look! There's a light burning beneath the door of the second form common room . . . and voices.
Daisy Burglars!
Trixie Shhh!
Daisy We must wake Miss Gibson.
Trixie And get into a frightful row for being here ourselves?
Daisy But surely we should consider school property before ourselves?
Trixie I daresay, you're right, Daisy, I'll go to Miss Gibson with you. But hold fire for a second or two . . .
Daisy Trixie!
Trixie Shhh! I'll take a tiny peep through the keyhole just to make sure.
Daisy Of what? What can you see?
Trixie (*giggling*) Oh Jemima! What a sell!
Daisy Can I have a look?
Trixie It's the second form up to their ears in a midnight feast. Let me have another peep, Daisy . . . doughnuts, toffee-apples, vanilla sandwiches . . . I've a good mind to go in there and demand a share for keeping quiet.

Clare enters quietly

Clare Trixie Martin! Daisy Meredith!
Both Clare!
Clare Perhaps you will both come and see me in my study tomorrow morning and inform me of the purpose behind this midnight visitation.
Trixie But Clare . . .
Clare I'll wake Miss Calder to deal with those babes. I'll see you both tomorrow.

Clare exits

Trixie Jemima! We're for it now.

Daisy Will Clare report us to Miss Gibson, do you think?

Trixie If she thinks we've been utterly evil, she might. No, the worst of it is, is whether the Second form recognized our voices or not. They'll think we were absolute sneaks if they did.

Daisy They wouldn't think that, would they?

Trixie How else could Clare have discovered them? What we've got to find out is, who sneaked on us!

Daisy and Trixie exit

Clare and Alice enter Clare's study

Clare ... if only you'd seen them, Alice, they looked so wonderfully comic dressed up in two of Matron's cloaks, supposed to be monks or something equally ghostly.

Alice How absolutely sublime.

Clare Yes, it was rather a hoot, though it gave me a perfect fright at first.

Alice Oh, Clare.

Clare What I'd like to know is how they got themselves involved in keeping watch for a Second form feast. The Fourth always look on the Seconds as such babes.

Alice Do you not remember the fine japes we used to get up to in our young days?

Clare What utter little horrors we were. Do you remember that winter we went on the midnight skating expedition ...

Alice ... and Katy Collins falling through the thin ice.

They fall about laughing. Knocking is heard on the study door

Clare Oh, here they are.

Alice I'll leave you to it, me darlin' girl, I've a flute lesson in town.

Clare See you on the field at one, Alice.

Alice Cheeriosa!

Clare Don't let Miss Gibson hear you slanging like that.

Alice exits, passing Daisy and Trixie on her way out

Come in, you two.

Daisy and Trixie enter

Now perhaps the pair of you will tell me why you took it upon yourselves last night to break a good many school-rules and at the same time risk getting the Second form into a jolly serious fix. Remember as Fourths you are responsible for setting a good example to the lower school, not leading them into situations which you know to be contrary to the rules of Grangewood.

Trixie We had nothing to do with the Seconds' feast, truly, Clare.

Daisy Honour bright.

Clare Then why on earth ...

Daisy The truth of the matter is, Clare, we were searching for the treasure,

the Beaumont treasure, and we were on our way to the East Gallery to rap
panels and all that kind of thing, when we stumbled across the Seconds
knocking off buns. We know that the East Gallery is out of bounds which
is why we disguised ourselves, but we're both dreadfully sorry.

Clare (*to the audience*) The corners of Clare's mouth twitched, and it was
with some effort that she hastily pulled herself together. I see.

Trixie We're immensely sorry for getting you up in the middle of the night
too.

Clare Well, I shan't report you to Miss Gibson . . .

Daisy
Trixie } (*together*) Oh, thanks most awfully, Clare.

Clare But as you, Trixie, have been here the longest and ought to know
better than to . . .

Daisy Please, Clare, it was my idea just as much as Trixie's.

Trixie Thank you, Daisy.

Clare Very well, on Saturday from lunch until teatime, you will both stay
within the confines of the school building.

Trixie Oh, but we shall miss the first knock-out match of the County
Hockey Championships.

Clare Well, my dear child, it's high time you gave up kiddish stunts.

Daisy Clare, is there any truth in the story of the Beaumont treasure?

Clare How serious are you both about finding it?

Daisy
Trixie } (*together*) Immensely serious.

Clare Then I will tell you—yes, the Beaumont treasure does exist.

Daisy and Trixie both gasp

You see, kiddies, the mystery centres around my grandfather, the late Sir
Digby Beaumont. Now, he was a tremendously eccentric gentleman, who,
as he got older, became more and more impatient with the new ideas and
as he thought, lower standards of the younger generation. This led to
endless arguments in the family, especially with the younger of his two
sons, my Uncle David, who left home after a particularly vehement
quarrel with Sir Digby and has never been seen or heard of since.

Trixie How fearful.

Clare Shortly after this awful quarrel, Sir Digby died and his wealth—all
manner of family heirlooms, money, valuables—disappeared. In his will it
was revealed that he had hidden this treasure somewhere within the walls
of Grangewood, and a set of clues leading to its whereabouts, so
complicated that the treasure can only be uncovered by whosoever has
wit enough to unravel these clues. My father hunted unceasingly for the
treasure right up until his death four years ago, but since then no-one's
had much impetus to carry on with the search. Oh, the will did say
another important clue lies with my Uncle David, but as he's been gone
twenty years or so, there's little hope there.

Daisy I was looking at the portraits of your family in the Great Hall and I
noticed that one of the frames was empty.

Clare Yes. Now that contained the only known portrait of my Uncle

David. My grandfather had it removed after the quarrel.
Trixie How perfectly tragic.
Daisy Was your grandfather a scientist?
Clare Why do you ask?
Daisy In his portrait he's holding a jolly queer looking instrument of some kind.
Clare It's a device apparently, for measuring the distances between stars, my grandfather was tremendously keen on astronomy.
Trixie How uncommonly rare.

A bell rings, off

Clare There goes the bell for end of break. Off you go, kiddies, and thank you most awfully for showing such an interest in the treasure.
Trixie I tell you, Clare, we mean to find it for you.
Clare Remember no more midnight expeditions.
Trixie We'll be perfect seraphs.
Daisy Honour bright.

Clare exits

Trixie What an out and out sport!
Daisy Clare is absolutely the most adorable girl I've ever met, I'd risk anything for her.
Trixie Except I wish she wouldn't call us kiddies.
Daisy Better than being called babes like the Firsts and Seconds.
Trixie I say, Daisy, did you notice how fearfully sad Clare looked—just for a moment—when she mentioned her father's death?
Daisy Yes, I know just how she jolly well feels.
Trixie Why, is your father . . .
Daisy Yes, ten years ago. He was a ship's doctor in the Royal Navy. He was reported missing, believed dead, when his ship went down in the Baltic during the Battle of . . .
Trixie I'm immensely sorry.
Daisy I was fearfully young of course, when it happened. I say, we must hurry. Miss Granville will be wild if we're late for her class.
Trixie I wish you'd slack off a bit Daisy, I'm sure you'll end up with brain fever if you carry on at this rate.

They enter the Form Room

O Jubilate, we're first in.
Daisy I say, look at that on the board, "We don't stand for sneaks at Grangewood, especially elementary ones".
Trixie Jemima! Someone risked their neck to write that.
Daisy It must be the Seconds, they recognized our voices last night.
Trixie Here come the others. Quick, the blackboard!

Daisy and Trixie rush towards the blackboard

Sybil, Monica, Belinda and Dora enter

Sybil Sneak.

Monica giggles

Elementary sneak.

Miss Granville enters

Miss Granville Good morning, girls.

Girls Good morning, Miss Granville.

Miss Granville Thank-you, Trixie and Daisy for cleaning the blackboard, but it really wasn't necessary to wipe off today's list of essay topics. Take an order mark each and return to your seats please. Now, I have here the essays handed in by you all last week on the subject of Shelley's poem, "Ode to the West Wind", some of which were extremely good and others which were lamentable to say the least. Dora Johnston, kindly refrain from rattling that ink-well. One essay, which I thought exceptional in content, I was forced to give half-marks to owing to the blots and inky fingerprints which almost obliterated it. If you are incapable, Daisy Meredith, of coping with a pen and ink, you will have to use a pencil. Let me see no more work like this.

Miss Granville holds up Daisy's book — the class gasps

Daisy But ...

Miss Granville Have you anything to say to me regarding the atrocious condition of this book, Daisy?

Daisy Yes, Miss Granville. I did not hand in my work in that condition, I give you my word.

Miss Granville Then your word cannot be worth very much, Daisy. Are you suggesting that these blots appeared of their own volition?

Daisy No ... I ...

Miss Granville Or are you perhaps suggesting someone else had a hand in creating this mess?

Sybil Sneak.

Daisy No ... I don't know. All I know is, that when I wrote my essay it was perfectly clear of any blots.

Miss Granville (*narrating*) Miss Granville hesitated ... she believed the morals if not the intellects of elementary schoolgirls to be lower than those of the type of girl normally to be found at Grangewood ... yet ... honesty shone forth from Daisy's face and the ring of truth was within her speech. (*To Daisy*) Very well, Daisy, I shall take your word for it this time, that you really believed that the essay you handed in was presentable, but I think that next time, perhaps, a little blotting paper would not come amiss. Now, who is this week's book monitor? Ah, Belinda, will you please return these exercise books to their owners. Thank you. Now girls, just a brief word on the topics for this year's School Poetry competition, details of which you will also find pinned to the notice-board. There are two subjects, from which you must choose one only; the first being "Heroes" Have you all got that? "Heroes". Belinda, have you a pencil-sharpener you can lend Dora Johnston, please? The second subject being a poem which must bear the title, "The Meditations of a Lighthouse". These poems must not exceed fifty lines in length and must be handed in by Friday week.

Daisy (*narrating*) Daisy found it a struggle to concentrate for the rest of that lesson. She was convinced that Sybil had had a hand in defacing her essay, for one of Sybil's responsibilities as Vice-Captain of the form was to collect prep-work and hand it in to the appropriate teacher, thereby giving her the opportunity to wreak any damage she chose. But how was she to prove it without committing the despicable sin of sneaking? If only Sybil didn't hate me so. Life would be absolute bliss if she and I were chums. I'm convinced she has some good in her, as most prickly pears have, but she mustn't be allowed to carry on her beastly stunts and to palter with the honour of the Upper Fourth or that of Grangewood. *Honesta quam magna. Hinc spes effulget.*

A bell rings off

  Miss Granville exits

Mr Thompson is heard whistling "All Through the Night" outside

Trixie There goes Mr Thompson with an immense basket of apples.

Dora Fearful shame that. I've been planning a raid on the orchard for days. Doesn't look as if there's any point now.

Sybil Honestly, I shall write to Mummy and Daddy about the frightful state Grangewood's rapidly sinking into. First sneaking scholarship girls, now thieving—

Trixie That's beastly unfair of you, Sybil.

Sybil The entire school is in a ferment. The Seconds have had their pocket money stopped for a fortnight and aren't to have any cakes or jam at tea for a week. Isn't that so, Monica?

Monica Entirely, Sybil, entirely.

Sybil Is it right that the honour of the Upper Fourth and the morals of one of its members, namely Trixie Martin, should be thrown into disrepute by one girl.

Belinda Rot, Sybil.

Monica You'll see if it's rot.

Trixie We all shall. Daisy and I will go and see the Seconds ourselves and tell them that whoever sneaked upon us was responsible for their discovery. And what's more, we intend to find the person responsible and expose her to the entire school.

Mr Scoblowski enters

Mr Scoblowski (*narrating*) At that moment, however, Mr Scoblowski entered the form room to commence his Geography lesson with the Fourth. (*To the pupils*) Good morning, girls.

Girls Good morning, Mr Scoblowski.

Mr Scoblowski Please open your Geography text books at page thiry-one. This morning we will study Peru.

Daisy (*narrating*) Daisy opened her book at the appropriate page and as she did so, a slip of printed paper fluttered from the book and on to the floor. Daisy paled as she picked it up, suddenly aware that Sybil Burlington had also read the words printed on the piece of paper.

Mr Scoblowski I will first of all announce the results of last Wednesday's Geography test, beginning from the bottom. Sybil Burlington—twenty-one out of one hundred marks. Dora Johnston—forty-eight. Monica Smithers—seventy-four. Trixie Martin—eighty-one. Belinda Mathieson—ninety-one. Daisy Meredith—ninety-three. Well done, especially Belinda and Daisy. Sybil, I am surprised at you, your marks are usually better than this. If they continue to be this appalling, I shall have you sent down to the First Form for Geography lessons.

Monica giggles. Sybil glares

Daisy (*narrating*) Geography was the second lesson that morning which failed to leave any impression upon Daisy's mind, which was whirling upon another matter far removed from the jungles and mountains of Peru.

A bell rings off

Mr Scoblowski You may put away your books now, girls. I would like to see in the main music-room this afternoon at four o'clock, those girls who are singing solo in the end of term concert. Thank you.

Mr Scoblowski exits followed by everyone else except Daisy and Sybil

Daisy (*narrating*) As the Upper Fourth prepared to go to lunch, Sybil Burlington caught Daisy's arm.

Sybil Look here, Daisy Meredith, unless you devise some means of getting yourself removed from Grangewood within the next fortnight, I shall tell Miss Gibson of what I saw, printed on that piece of paper.

Daisy (*narrating*) For the piece of paper to which Sybil referred had printed upon it the answers to the previous Wednesday's Geography test.

Sybil And we don't stand for cheats at Grangewood.

CURTAIN

ACT II

In the darkness schoolgirl voices are heard chanting

Voices   A tongue like a snake, a beak like a drake
A cheat like a cat and a sneak like a rat!

Daisy Meredith is a funny one
She's got a face like a pickled onion
A nose like a squashed tomato
And two bandy legs.

The Lights come up in the common room where Trixie is finishing her poem and Daisy is darning a sock

Daisy I say, Trixie, when do you suppose the Seconds will give up this sneaking and cat-calling stunt?

Trixie In a week or two, if they've any sense of honour. They have rather got their knives into you, old girl. I suppose Sybil's been feeding them all this elementary school bilge. She and Monica went out on to the field this afternoon looking like queens of tragedy. They absolutely detest games—sure sign of a rotter.

Daisy I wonder how the match is going, it's jolly sickening not to know which side the cheers are for.

Trixie I would have gone without cakes and jam for a year just to have seen the match and Clare's playing.

Mr Thompson is heard whistling "All Through the Night", off

I say, Daisy, will you let me read your poem when it's finished?

Daisy I'm fearfully sorry, Trixie, old chum, but no. Please don't be offended but I think it's tremendously bad form to show competition entries to one's fellow competitors, it can lead to colossal temptation.

Trixie I understand perfectly, Daisy, old thing, I think it's a thoroughly decent idea.

Daisy I haven't even begun mine yet, though I will say that my choice of title is "The Meditations of a Lighthouse".

Trixie Mine's the jolly old "Heroes". I've practically finished.

Daisy (*finishing the darning*) There, that's done, Matron ought to be well satisfied. I say, what shall we do now?

Trixie Beastly boring being shut up in here. I know, let's treasure-hunt, let's revive the Dark Horse Secret Society.

Daisy Topping idea! Where do you suggest we begin our search?

Trixie Not along the East Gallery, that's for certain. Have to wait until we're prefects to get down there.

Daisy Look here, Trixie, we need ideas, let's go to the library and see if we can find any books about other treasure-seekers, or a book on codes or even a biography of Sir Digby Beaumont.

Trixie Capital suggestion. Let's go down the back stairs, less chance of Matron or any of the maids seeing us.

Daisy Why? Is the library normally out of bounds?

Trixie Yes, unless there's a prefect or mistress in there. But we didn't promise Clare not to go in the library, did we? I say, someone's coming . . . quick . . . hide down here.

They hide as Mr Scoblowski enters with a notebook and pencil furiously making notes about the ancestral portraits in the hall

Trixie almost sneezes out loud, but Daisy stops her by putting her hand over Trixie's mouth

Phew! That was a near thing. I say, Daisy, why do you suppose he's writing such volumes about the ancestral portraits?

Daisy I can't say for certain, but I've a pretty good idea . . .

Trixie Daisy, you don't suppose . . .

Mr Scoblowski exits

Daisy That's just the point, Trixie, old chum, I do.

Trixie I wonder how much he knows that we don't . . . perhaps we should tell Clare or Miss Gibson what we suspect.

Daisy No, Trixie, we must solve this ourselves. I put you on your honour not to divulge a single word about our hunt to anyone from now on, not even to Clare or Miss Gibson, until we find the treasure.

Trixie I won't breathe a syllable . . . even if it means missing the next hockey knockout.

Daisy Trixie, you're a trump.

Trixie Daisy, that's queer, look at that device that the old fellow, Sir Digby's holding, seems to sort of . . . stand out from the rest of the picture.

Daisy Brighter shade of paint than the rest, that's all. Come on, to the library . . . so many books, it's frightfully difficult to know where to look.

Trixie Heaps of biographies over here . . .

Daisy Here's a volume on codes and ciphers.

Trixie Here's one by the old boy himself. Hey, there's lots of them . . . most of them seem to be about astronomy.

Daisy Let's find every one of them we can, we've stacks of time to look through them all.

Trixie Well, those are all of Sir Digby's books that I can find.

Daisy Right, now we must scour absolutely every page of every book. We're looking for sheets of paper slipped in between the pages, scribbled notes in the margin, that kind of thing.

Trixie My goodness, Daisy, you have got brains.

Daisy You've not so prodigiously few yourself.

Daisy and Trixie look through the books

Alice and Clare enter, carrying hockey sticks

Alice How's Diana?

Clare She's definitely out now for the second half—Matron will never let her play with a broken ankle.

Alice The vantage is ours.

Clare I'm not so jolly certain, Alice.

Alice We're leading by six goals to one.

Clare That goalie of Thorphurst's is first-rate, I've had umpteen pots at the goal, but Diana was the only girl able to get one in.

Alice Julia is a jolly decent substitute.

Clare Can't afford to get complacent, Alice.

A whistle blows, off

There goes the whistle for the second half. Watch that left inner, Alice.

Alice I'll stick to her like a shadow.

Clare and Alice exit

Trixie If we don't find a clue, I shall simply expire.

Daisy *Hinc spes effulget.*

Trixie It'd be such a mean horrid beastly sell if we didn't.

Pause

I say, Daisy, listen to this . . .
> My first is above where cherubim reign
> My second in Sagittarius nickname
> My third in . . .

Daisy Let me see.

Trixie Some joker defacing school property.

Daisy But Trixie, don't you see . . .?

Trixie See what?

Daisy This is it . . . what we've been searching for . . . the clue!

Trixie O Jubilate! Jemima! Someone's coming this way.

Daisy Quick, underneath the table.

They get under the library table

Trixie The book! (*She grabs the book*)

A second later Mr Scoblowski enters. He sees the books and examines them

Mr Scoblowski Goodness gracious . . . Sir Digby Beaumont . . . I wonder.

Belinda enters

Belinda Mr Scoblowski! Mr Scoblowski! Mr Thompson's here to see you.

Mr Scoblowski Dash it!

Mr Scoblowski and Belinda exit

Trixie That proves it, it jolly well proves it, he's after the treasure! I wonder if Mr Thompson has anything to do with it, I've noticed that he and Mr Scoblowski are pretty thick together.

Daisy Trixie, let's copy this clue down before Mr Scoblowski returns.

Trixie I say, Daisy let's tear the page out so that Mr Scoblowski can't find it.

Daisy We can't deface school property.

Trixie Let's take the whole book then.

Daisy That would be stealing.

Trixie Not really it wouldn't, we'd only be borrowing it . . . it's for the sake of the school.

Daisy Well, I don't know . . .

Trixie And Clare.

Daisy Right-o!

Trixie O Jubilate, Daisy, I knew you'd see sense.

Daisy Let's put all these other books away then, quickly.

Daisy and Trixie return the books to the shelves

Mr Scoblowski (*off*) Well, I will see you this evening—I have not the time now, I'm extremely busy.

Trixie Daisy, he's coming back! Quick, up the stairs!

Mr Scoblowski I have a Geography lesson to prepare—I'm sorry, I'm sorry.

Mr Scoblowski enters, and sees the books are no longer there

H'mm, h'mm.

Mr Scoblowski exits

Daisy Phew! In the nick of time. Now for that clue.

Trixie Read it out, Daisy.

Daisy   My first is above where cherubim reign.
      My second in Sagittarius nickname.
      My third in the eighth of Saturn's great brood
      My fourth is in Aries and doth provide food
      My fifth at the end of the first planet lies
      My sixth spangles brightly the late evening skies
      My seventh lies in the beast that the starry twins follow
      My eighth the north night skies with brave colours swallow
      My last lies in the hue of the warrior planet
      And there if you read me aright you will have it.
      Take my initials in the order they're writ
      And your way to the final clue will be lit.
I say, Trixie, how glorious.

Trixie A real clue! Quick, we must work it out. (*She writes down the answers to the clues*)

Daisy My first is above where cherubim reign . . . well that's easy enough . . . Heaven.

Trixie So H is our first letter. The second is A for Archer . . . Sagittarius.

Daisy Wise child. My third is the eighth of Saturn's great brood . . . here's a conundrum, I didn't know Saturn had any children.

Trixie Didn't think he had a wife.
Daisy Think, Trixie, think.
Trixie I'm racking my brains. A dictionary of astronomy, that's what we need.
Daisy Trixie, this book's got a glossary.
Trixie Uncommonly handy.
Daisy Scorpio . . . Sirius . . . Star-gazer . . . Saturn! Saturn, rings, distance from earth, moons . . . moons! Moons! Brood!
Trixie The eighth, what's the name of the eighth moon?
Daisy Iapetus.
Trixie I. Next?
Daisy My fourth is in Aries and doth provide food . . . ah, Aries the Ram.
Trixie We're getting on famously. Hair we've got.
Daisy My fifth at the end of the first planet lies . . . Mercury . . . Y.
Trixie I say! Hairy!
Daisy Hairy?
Trixie 'Swat it says.
Daisy My sixth spangles brightly the late evening skies . . .
Trixie Stars! S!
Daisy Topping, Trixie. Now the beast that the starry twins follow . . .
Trixie Pollux and Castor . . . Taurus the Bull! Taurus!
Daisy My eighth the north night skies with brave colours swallow. North? Why north I wonder?
Trixie I know, Northern Lights. Aurora something . . . Aurora borry . . .
Daisy Never mind, we've got the A. My last lies in the hue of the Warrior Planet.
Trixie Mars! Red! It's red!
Daisy And there if you read me aright you will have it.
Trixie Hairy star.
Daisy Doesn't make sense.
Trixie Have a look in the glossary.
Daisy Nothing about hairy stars in here. Trixie, perhaps we've got it wrong.
Trixie Perhaps it's an astronomical symbol.
Daisy Queer sort of symbol.
Trixie Perhaps Sir Digby was a lunatic.

Monica and Sybil's voices are heard off

Daisy Voices! The match must be over.
Trixie We must hide the book.
Daisy Where?
Trixie In your boot-hole. Hairy star, don't forget it, Daisy, hairy star.

Trixie and Daisy exit

Sybil and Monica enter, Monica carrying a bag of buns

Monica I say, Sybil, are you sure no-one can see us?
Sybil Honestly, Monica, you really are green sometimes. Everyone's too taken up with the match to notice our absence.

Monica Here are the buns. I'm afraid, Sybil, they're the tiniest bit damp, it's muddy in the tea-tent.

Sybil I bag the creamy one.

They eat the buns

Monica Isn't this blissful?

Sybil How wild they'd all be if they could see us—instead of swiping at their silly balls.

Monica Especially Daisy Meredith.

Sybil All swank, she's hopeless really. Fearfully good idea of yours, that Geography paper, Monica.

Monica You inspired it, Sybil. It would have been nothing without you to carry it through.

Sybil I fear for Grangewood if the Meredith girl remains to taint it for very much longer. Clare and the mistresses are ready to kiss her boots at present, but they'll soon change their tune especially when my next scheme comes to fruition.

Monica Oh Sybil, I do think you have the most gorgeous character of anyone I know.

Sybil I daresay you're right. Come on, I want to finish my poem.

Sybil and Monica exit

Clare (*off*) Three cheers for Thorphurst, the gallant losers. Hip, hip . . .

There is cheering off

Clare and Alice enter, exhausted

What a dickens of a game.

Alice Sure, I didn't know if I was coming or going.

Clare How's your shin, Alice?

Alice Bruised—like a thunder cloud. 'Tis a sight better I'll be bound than Diana's ankle . . .

Clare Or Carol's knee . . .

Alice Or Jane's cracked rib.

Clare I scarcely like to think about the team we will have to scrape together for the next match.

Alice And the final, if we reach it.

Clare Still, buck up, old thing, there are some jolly decent players in the Fifth.

Alice Have you not remembered, Clare, that in the week of the finals the Fifth are away in France.

Clare 'Nuff said. That leaves the Fourth—Belinda, Trixie and the new girl. Chin-up, Alice, a miracle may happen and our injured may recover in time to play. Let's wash and change, then go and cheer up the wounded soldiers in the San.

There is a shriek, off

My word, it's Mademoiselle.

Mademoiselle enters

Mademoiselle (*to the audience*) Mademoiselle, the scatter-brained French mistress of Grangewood. (*To Clare and Alice*) Tiens! C'est abominable! A thief 'as been in ze library and taken a most valuable book. It is I who am to blame n'est-ce pas. For I am on library duty this week.

Clare Steady on, Mademoiselle, are you absolutely sure the book has been stolen?

Mademoiselle Positive. For I come in to see zat all is well after ze splendid 'ockey match and pouf! I see a big gap on ze shelf.

Clare Which book was it, Mademoiselle, can you remember?

Mademoiselle Mais oui! It belonged to your esteemed grandpère and was about ze stars in ze 'eavens. I 'ave looked at it often in great wonder. I must find Miss Gibson and tell 'er what 'as occurred.

Clare I'll come with you, Mademoiselle, for this concerns me very much. See you in the San, Alice.

Clare and Mademoiselle exit

Alice Things are lookin' black for you indeed, me darlin' girl.

Alice exits

Everyone enters for Assembly, singing the hymn "Lord of all Hopefulness"

Trixie (*to Daisy*) I found this in the dormy, it's addressed to you.

Daisy (*narrating*) Reluctantly Daisy opened the envelope, a feeling of grim foreboding stealing over her. Sybil Burlington's spidery handwriting revealed itself . . . "one week or Grangewood will know the truth about the Geography paper". Daisy paled.

Trixie I say, Daisy, bad news?

Daisy (*to Trixie*) No, I've a headache. (*Narrating*) That Geography paper— how had it come to be in her desk? Daisy half-suspected Sybil of the deed except that the look of surprise on the girl's face had seemed genuine. How she longed to make a clean breast of the affair to Miss Gibson or Clare—but who would believe the word of an elementary schoolgirl in the face of such condemning evidence and against that of a wealthy, beautiful self-assured Grangewood scholar, especially one who desired her departure so keenly. (*To herself*) But I can't leave Grangewood, I love it so and mother would be tremendously upset. I know, I'll destroy the Geography paper then no-one need be any the wiser. Why on earth didn't I think of that sooner?

Miss Gibson Now we come to the morning's notices. The match on Saturday against Thorphurst was won, as you all know, by Grangewood six–three.

Everyone cheers

A splendid effort by all concerned—which means that Grangewood goes through to the semi-final. Several injuries were sustained by our players which means that the First Eleven will be on the look-out for possible substitutes for the next match, and the final, if we are fortunate enough to reach it. This of course, will give members of the Fifth and Fourth forms a chance to show their mettle.

Daisy How topping.

Trixie How scrummy.

Miss Gibson A list of those girls being considered is pinned on the school notice-board. I have been informed that several girls on their way to specialized music lessons in the town have been observed conversing with boys from St Hugo's County Grammar School. This must stop. Mingling with brothers, cousins and boys at supervised social events is perfectly in order, but this casual hob-nobbing can do nothing but harm to Grangewood's reputation. A nature-ramble to Pebble Cove will be led by Miss Waller on Sunday afternoon for any girls interested—names in by Wednesday please. Finally, I come to a matter of the utmost gravity. A book of astronomy, part of the Sir Digby Beaumont Collection, has been taken—I hesitate to say stolen—from the school library. We believe it to have been purloined by someone who possibly does not realize that books may not be taken from the library without express permission from either myself or the mistress-in-charge for that week. If the person who has the book would care to come and see me privately this morning, I will say nothing about the matter. However, if no-one owns up, afternoon games will be cancelled ...

Everyone gasps

... and the entire school kept within bounds for the next three days.

Everyone gasps again

School dismissed.

All exit except for Daisy and Trixie

Trixie We really are in deadly peril now. What atrocious luck that the book should be missed so soon.

Daisy If we hand it back, Mr Scoblowski is sure to discover the clue.

Trixie I say, Daisy, do you think he suspects that we're the culprits, after all, we've actually told him that we're looking for the treasure.

Daisy He may sneak on us.

Trixie Oh, Daisy, how frightful. Perhaps we should chuck the whole affair in.

Daisy And let the Bolsheviks get their hands on the treasure?

Trixie You're right, Daisy, for the sake of the school ...

Daisy ... and England. No, we must keep extremely quiet about the whole affair and admit to nothing.

Trixie *Honesta quam magna.*

Trixie }
Daisy } *(together) Hinc spes effulget.*

Girls enter and gather around the school notice-board

Trixie I say, look at the crowd around the notice-board. Let us through,

Winnie. Daisy! You and I and Belinda are all down for the hockey trials on Thursday.

Daisy How spiffing.

Winnie Even more spiffing if someone returns that beastly book and we get our three games periods back.

Trixie I say, Daisy, where are you off to?

Daisy I left something in my desk.

Trixie Right-o!

The Girls and Trixie exit

Daisy enters the classroom

Daisy Now to destroy that Geography paper. (*She looks in her desk*) It's gone!

Monica enters

Monica Sybil asked me to tell you that she's borrowed your Geography text book for prep. But here, I'll lend you mine.

Monica exits

Daisy The beasts! I sometimes wish I'd never heard of Grangewood. But I'll show them, I'll show them what the Merediths are made of . . . I'll show you, Sybil Burlington. Tell who you like about the Geography paper, I'll not admit to something that isn't my fault, I'll not submit to blackmail. I'm staying at Grangewood—yes, until the Sixth form, Sybil Burlington, until the Sixth form.

Trixie enters

Trixie Come on, Daisy, we'd better cut along to the lab.

Winnie Irving enters

Winnie (*to the audience*) Winnie Irving, a member of the Second Form. (*To Daisy*) I say, Daisy Meredith?

Daisy Yes?

Winnie I've a message for you from the Second and First forms—we don't stand for sneaks at Grangewood and until such time as you either apologize to us for your low behaviour, reform or leave the school, we are sending you and Trixie Martin to Coventry.

Winnie exits

Trixie I'd like to wipe the ground with the cheeky little beggar.

Daisy I sometimes think that Grangewood is a perfectly horrible, miserable school.

Trixie You need bucking-up, old chum. (*Pause*) Got it! I'll arrange an inter-dormy bottle-fight.

Daisy What's that?

Trixie It's like a pillow-fight but with hot-water bottles. You fill them half-full of water for extra suppleness and then bang! You're off. It's a prime stunt. We'll do it tomorrow night after prayers when the Prees are having their baths.

Daisy Sounds a topping idea, I feel better already.

Whistling of "All Through the Night" is heard, off

What is the name of that tune that Mr Thompson always whistles, do you know, Trixie?

Trixie Dash it, I can't think . . . a Welsh song, you should know it, Daisy . . . *All Through the Night*, that's the one.

Daisy It's queer, Trixie, but it's frightfully reminiscent of something.

Trixie Your mater probably sang it to you when you were but an infant on her knee.

Daisy And he always whistles the same tune.

Trixie Slightly cracked, poor old chap, so they say. Avoids people like the plague.

A bell rings off

I say, we'll be late for Science if we don't dash.

Trixie dashes off

Daisy takes a book from her desk and goes to follow Trixie

Mr Scoblowski enters

Daisy bumps into Mr Scoblowski

Daisy Excuse me, Mr Scoblowski, I'm late for a class.

Mr Scoblowski Ah, I hope it is not because you were treasure-hunting!

Daisy No, we've given up all that ever since we discovered that only juniors believe in the treasure.

Mr Scoblowski (*narrating*) Mr Scoblowski was not convinced, however. (*He grabs Daisy's arm*) I know very well that you and the other girl have the book hidden away . . .

Daisy Ow! Mr Scoblowski, you're hurting my arm.

Mr Scoblowski But I intend to find it! It is imperative, you do not realize . . .

Trixie enters

Trixie I say, Daisy, are you coming? What the . . .

Mr Scoblowski exits

Daisy!

Daisy He knows we've got the book.

Trixie There's only one thing for it, we must discover the secret of the hairy star!

Trixie and Daisy exit

A clock chimes nine

Monica enters in her dressing-gown and sits and reads a comic. Sybil enters carrying a book

Sybil Monica!

Monica Sybil!

Sybil I've just discovered this in Daisy Meredith's boot-hole. (*Pause*) It's the book, Monica.

Monica How absolutely splendid.

Sybil How despicably low. I'll replace it and leave you, Monica, to see that the proper persons are informed.

Monica They will be, Sybil, they will be.

Sybil exits with the book

Girls, including Daisy and Trixie, enter having a bottle-fight. Sybil returns and joins in the fight

Alice enters

Alice Daisy Meredith! Just what are you doing with that hot-water bottle? Kindly remove it . . . and the rest of you children can return to whichever dormy you belong to, at once! Inter-dormy bottle-fights, I wonder who thought of that one.

Sybil But you used to—

Alice Yes, I know we used to do it at your age, but we took great care not to get caught.

Belinda We thought all the Precs were having baths.

Alice We can't all get in at the same time. Enough of this ragging, an order mark to any girl who's not in her own dormy by the time I've counted to ten. Sybil Burlington, please wait in my study, I wish to have a word with you.

Alice and the other girls exit

Daisy and Trixie join Monica

Daisy Phew! Alice is in a pixie mood.

Trixie A regular sport though, always gives one a chance. I had an absolutely scrummy tussle with Jill Timms and Rosie Wildgust from the Third and then Jill's hot-water bottle burst!

Daisy Matron will be frightfully fed-up about that.

Trixie Oh, Matron's a sport, she'll gather the joyful gist.

"All Through the Night" is heard being whistled outside

Daisy Why didn't you join in the bottle-fight, Monica?

Monica I'm not feeling well.

Daisy Let's play a game to jolly you up, we've heaps of time before lights out.

Trixie That's a topping idea, Daisy.

Daisy How about a game we all know, I know—the Dictionary Game.

Trixie Right-o!

Daisy Here we are, pencils, paper and a small pocket dictionary. (*She hands the pencils and paper round*)

Trixie Goodness, what amazing pockets.

Daisy I've a penknife, string and coughsweets as well. My four brothers are

Boy Scouts you see, and their motto is "Be Prepared" for any emergency.
Trixie I bags to be first on it.
Daisy No, Trixie, I bags to be first on it.
Trixie Right-o. You do know how to play, don't you Monica?
Monica Of course I do.
Trixie First word, Daisy?
Daisy First word, well it's a name really . . . hairy star.
Trixie Hairy star?
Daisy Hairy star.
Trixie There's no such word.
Monica Yes, there is. I'm not quite sure I can remember what it means.

They write down their definitions

Daisy Right-o, all done? Hand them over. Now a hairy star . . . is a species
of fungus found growing under beech trees, a Colonial term for the Union
Jack, or a comet so-called in ancient times because its fiery tail resembled
that of a—

Alice enters

Alice Well, well, this is a cosy little confab. Did you not hear me call for
lights out?
Daisy No, sorry Alice, we didn't.
Monica Sybil's our dormy monitor, don't we have to wait for her to tell us?
Alice Sybil's with me for the minute. Now off you all run to your beds.
Monica Good-night, Alice.
Alice Good-night, Monica.
Trixie 'Night, Alice.
Alice Good-night, Trixie.
Daisy Good . . .
Alice Daisy, can I speak with you for a minute?
Daisy Yes.

Trixie and Monica exit

Alice Are you well, child, you've been looking a wee bit pale of late?
Daisy I'm in splendid form, thank you, Alice.
Alice You've been sleeping at nights?
Daisy Like the proverbial log.
Alice I think I'll ask Matron to dose you up on cod-liver oil for a while.
Daisy Look here, Alice . . .
Alice You're too peaky looking for my liking and besides, we need fighters
not wraithes in the First Eleven. But it's not that I wish to speak to you of.
In the midst of that battle you were all engaged in ten minutes ago, a
Junior passed me on her way to the San sporting a black eye she'd
received in the onslaught. She'd been set upon by a crowd led by Sybil
Burlington, for refusing to join them in a foray against the Sneak of the
Fourth, as I believe you're known. Now, does this have anything to do
with the fact that when Clare pounced on you and Trixie that night she
also happed upon the Seconds feasting, who now see you as a sneak?

Daisy I'd rather not say, Alice.

Alice I've no intention of fighting any battles on your behalf, child, but right must be seen to exist where it does. Would you like me to have a discreet word with the Seconds?

Daisy No. Thanks awfully, Alice, but I mean to settle this on my own account.

Alice Are you sure, child?

Daisy Absolutely.

Alice Very well, off you run to bed then, kiddie.

Daisy Alice . . .

Alice Yes, child?

Daisy You aren't rowing Sybil on my account, are you?

Alice No, rest assured. I can't allow anyone, least of all a Vice-Captain of a form, to run around the school dishing out black eyes to all and sundry. Young Sybil will be on her way to Miss Gibson if she crosses my path again.

Daisy I say.

Alice Good-night, child.

Daisy Good-night, Alice.

Alice exits

Trixie rushes on

Trixie Oh, Daisy, the hairy star!

Daisy I know, oh Trixie, how glorious!

Trixie How uncommonly brainy of you to think up such a scheme . . .

Daisy How tremendously decent of Monica.

Trixie We must act at once, before Mr Scoblowski.

Daisy Tomorrow.

Trixie Tomorrow.

Daisy
Trixie } *(together) Hinc spes effulget.*

Everyone enters for Assembly, singing the hymn, "Let Us With a Gladsome Mind"

Miss Gibson The morning's notices. I learnt with great displeasure from Matron this morning that not a few girls have reported to her with burst hot-water bottles, the result it would seem of a dormitory prank. In future, all hot-water bottles similarly destroyed will be replaced with the aid of contributions from pocket-money. Persistent offenders will be relieved of their hot-water bottles and given hot bricks wrapped in flannel to take to bed. Now on to more pleasant matters. Grangewood has reached the final of the County Hockey Championships . . .

Everyone cheers

. . . and will meet Vearncombe Young Ladies College next Saturday for the match which will be played here on Grangewood's own hockey pitch.

Everyone cheers

Owing to the Fifth form's enforced absence from school this week, any substitutes required will be selected by Clare from the Fourth form. Not the happiest circumstances under which to meet such leviathans as Vearncombe, but remember girls, that even if we lose this very vital match, as long as you play the game, to the best of your very considerable abilities, you will not have failed Grangewood. Finally, it gives me tremendous delight to announce the results of this year's School Poetry Competition. While many of the entries were worthy of high commendation, all credit this year must go to the Upper Fourth who have produced the two winning entries. In second place we have "The Meditations of a Lighthouse" submitted by Sybil Burlington.

There is applause

Trixie My word! What a stunner!
Miss Gibson . . . and this year's winning entry is a poem on the subject of "Heroes" penned by Daisy Meredith.

There is applause

Trixie I say, well done.
Daisy But Trixie, I didn't . . .
Miss Gibson Quiet girls, please. I now take great pleasure in reading an extract from this indeed excellent piece of work. "Heroes" by Daisy Meredith.
> Through centuries wrapped in clouds of black
> Where injustice cruel doth rage
> There sometimes glows a candle bright
> That darkness to assuage.

Daisy Trixie! Please listen . . .
Miss Gibson   Poor folk crushed by tyrant's hand
> Of privilege bereft—

Trixie If you please, Miss Gibson—
Miss Gibson I am available in my study after Assembly for question or comment, Trixie Martin.
Trixie I'm sorry, Miss Gibson, but that poem you are reading out was not written by Daisy Meredith. I wrote it.

There is a gasp from the Girls

Miss Gibson Is this correct, Daisy?
Daisy Yes, Miss Gibson.
Miss Gibson Is this your handwriting, Trixie?
Trixie Yes, Miss Gibson.
Miss Gibson Most odd, and yet it has Daisy's name written upon it.
Daisy On my honour, Miss Gibson, I honestly had no idea . . . oh Trixie, surely you don't believe . . .
Miss Gibson Silence if you please, girls, silence. Trixie, I'll speak to you in a moment. Daisy Meredith, you are to go to my study and wait for me there.
Daisy But Miss Gibson . . .

Miss Gibson Please go. School dismissed.

Daisy exits. Everyone disperses

Belinda (*to Trixie*) What a beastly business! I would never have thought Daisy capable of such a frightful plot.

Miss Gibson Thank you, Belinda.

Belinda exits

(*To Trixie*) Don't worry, Trixie, we'll sort this out. Off you go.

Trixie exits

Daisy and Miss Gibson enter Miss Gibson's study

Daisy, this kind of affair grieves me intensely, especially when it concerns a girl in whom so much faith and expectation has been placed and whose academic and sporting future looked so bright. Now you say that you had no idea that Trixie Martin's poem was submitted under your name?

Daisy None at all, on my honour, Miss Gibson.

Miss Gibson And yet the name Daisy Meredith inscribed on the top of the entry compares remarkably well with other examples of your signature.

Daisy But Miss Gibson, I would never do such a thing to Trixie, she's my best chum.

Miss Gibson Not even in fun?

Daisy Not even in fun, Miss Gibson.

Miss Gibson A certain member of your form, I shall not mention her name, came to me with your Geography text book in which I found this—a printed list of answers to a Geography test set some time ago in which you came out top.

Daisy Miss Gibson, honestly, I had no idea . . . I didn't see it until . . .

Miss Gibson And this . . . (*She produces the astronomy book*) . . . was discovered at the back of your boot-hole.

Daisy I borrowed it, I can't tell you why, it's a point of honour, Miss Gibson, but I swear to you I had absolutely nothing to do with the poem or the Geography test.

Miss Gibson I must say, Daisy, I find it extremely difficult to believe anything of a girl who remained silent whilst her school-fellows suffered the loss of three days games and confinement to school grounds because of something she had not the courage to own up to. A girl also blind to the distress that this seeming theft has caused to the Beaumont family, particularly Clare.

Daisy I would never do anything to hurt Clare, Miss Gibson.

Miss Gibson I can only conclude, my dear, that perhaps we have demanded a little too much of you. The gulf between such schools as Grangewood and the elementary kind may be wider than we dream and I see the events of the past few weeks being as much my fault as yours, in having placed you under the tremendous pressures resulting in the matters now under discussion.

Daisy I'm awfully sorry, Miss Gibson, but as far as academic work and games go, I have not found myself under any of the tremendous pressures you mention, neither am I conscious of any enormous gulf between Grangewood and my previous school, as you are, if the gulf you speak of is mainly moral as you seem to imply. The only pressures I have encountered here are those from girls who because they have money, therefore have influence, a remarkably queer notion to my mind, and whose only code of conduct is that of lying, sneaking and bullying, and seeing fit to wipe the ground with me because in my ignorant elementary school way, I try to live up to the high standards set here, and to their irritation, succeed.

Miss Gibson That will do, Daisy Meredith. I shall attempt to get to the bottom of the accusations against you and will report my findings along with an academic and character assessment on you, to a meeting of the School Governors, to be held next Monday, when it will be decided whether or not, to keep you on at Grangewood. Until that time you will be given a room in the Sanatorium where you will sleep, your meals will be brought to you and you will be given specially prepared classwork to do. You will not be allowed to speak to any of your school-fellows or they to you, only to myself, teaching staff and Matron. You will be in Matron's charge and she will also arrange for your recreation periods. You may go.

Daisy Miss Gibson, on my honour, I swear I am innocent of the charges laid against me.

Miss Gibson exits

Daisy goes into the Sanatorium and throws herself on a bed

Oh mother, mother . . . oh Clare, if only I could explain to you . . . and Trixie . . . but now I never shall.

Trixie enters

Trixie Psst!
Daisy Trixie.
Trixie Oh, Daisy!
Daisy You'll get into fearful trouble if they find you here.
Trixie I know. It's perfectly beastly, we've been ordered not to speak to you on pain of death.
Daisy Oh Trixie, do you absolutely wish to goodness you'd never even met me? Do you believe I entered your poem as mine?
Trixie No, old chum, not for so much as a minute. I'm immensely sorry I spoke out in Assembly and not to Miss Gibson in private, I'm afraid I lost my rag.
Daisy I would have done exactly the same in your position though it's fearfully hard not to be dismal when everyone else believes I did do it. They found Sir Digby's book you know, I suppose Clare detests me now.
Trixie The book! Mr Scoblowski! The treasure! Daisy, we must stop him!
Daisy How? I'm not supposed to leave this room except to go to piano practise.
Trixie I'm not supposed to be in it. I'll work out some sort of a scheme . . . I'll also find out who rigged the poetry competition.

Daisy Probably someone's idea of a joke.

Trixie Queer sort of a joke. There are fearful rumours too, about you cribbing for a Geography test. What is the truth, Daisy?

Daisy I'm afraid I can't say, I'm not a sneak whatever else I may be.

Trixie It wouldn't surprise me if Sybil Burlington didn't have a hand in this somewhere.

A bell goes, off

Dash it, there goes the bell.

Daisy I'm so glad you don't absolutely loathe me, Trixie.

Trixie Buck-up, Daisy, old girl, I'll get you out of this piggy little mess, see if I don't.

Daisy Thanks awfully, Trixie. I must go to piano practice.

Trixie I'll creep up and see you later. Cheeriosa.

Daisy ⎫
Trixie ⎭ (*together*) *Hinc spes effulget.*

Trixie and Daisy exit

Clare and Alice enter

Clare Two days to the final, Diana's still out, Carol's hurt her knee again, and the Fifth away. It's no use, Alice, we shall have to put in some of those babes from the Fourth.

Trixie enters and stops to eavesdrop

Alice It's two we shall need.

Clare And if we're to beat Vearncombe this year, they've got to be good.

Alice There's Trixie Martin, splendid little player when she puts her mind to it.

Clare Belinda Mathieson.

Alice She's decent.

Clare Well, that's our team.

Beautiful piano playing is suddenly heard

Who's that who plays so beautifully?

Alice The wee girl, Daisy Meredith.

Clare A mistress surely.

Alice No, Daisy Meredith. Matron allows her to practise when a music-room lies empty.

Clare Poor child, anyone who plays like that cannot surely be guilty of the things she's been accused of.

Alice It's my belief she isn't.

Clare If only we had proof, Alice. I must say, I've noticed that certain elements in the school have done their best to make life tough for that kiddie.

Alice Can we not find that proof?

Clare We haven't much time, the School Governors meet to discuss her fate on Monday. I suppose we could have a jolly good go at clearing her name though.

Alice Even though she did walk off with your grandfather's book . . . and
deprived the school of three days' games.

Clare I was awfully fed-up about that, I admit.

Alice Daisy told Miss Gibson she held back on a point of honour . . . and
I'll tell you something now, I don't believe that a girl like Daisy who loves
her games would hold back for less.

Clare She's always struck me as a frightfully decent kid.

Trixie exits

Alice And don't you find it queer now, that such a girl should deliberately
set out to ruin herself? And to expose herself as a cheat and a leech upon
her best friend.

Clare That settles it, Alice, we will carry out our own investigation into this
affair. Thank you, old thing, for reminding me that as well as being
Games Captain of Grangewood, I am Head Girl.

Alice Sure, it's a deputy's duty.

There is a sudden shrieking and commotion off, and the piano playing stops

Clare I say, what a row.

Belinda enters

Belinda It's Trixie Martin, she's twisted her ankle. I'm going to find
Matron.

Belinda exits

Alice Jesus, Mary and Joseph!

Clare There goes another member of our First Eleven.

Alice *Nil desperandum*, me darlin' Clare.

Clare We're sunk. Might as well hand the trophy over to Vearncombe now.

Alice We'll find another substitute.

Clare Who else is there good enough?

Daisy's piano playing suddenly surges forth

Alice Wee Daisy Meredith.

Clare Do you think Miss Gibson will be persuaded?

Alice She must—for the sake of the school.

Clare and Alice exit

Daisy enters the San with a hockey stick, Trixie follows on crutches

They knock a hockey ball about between them

Trixie Goal!

Daisy Shhh. Matron will hear you and pack you off back to jolly old bed.

Trixie And deprive me of the chance of seeing you play for Grangewood?
Fat chance. She'd have the dickens of a deadly fight on her hands.

Daisy I say, Trixie, I'm horribly afraid I shall prove the most frightful muff.

Trixie You haven't muffed any practice games.

Daisy This is different. We shall be playing an absolutely first-class team not just eleven substitutes, and I feel I must justify Clare and Alice's faith in me after the tremendously hard job they must have had persuading Miss Gibson to let me play. I say, do you think any of the Grangewood girls will let on that one of their team is under threat of expulsion?

Trixie They wouldn't be such a pack of mean cats. If anyone, even that reptile, Sybil Burlington, uttered a word, I would cold-pig them every morning 'til the end of term.

Daisy I say, would you really?

Trixie With immense gratification. I say, it's capital the two of us being here in the San.

Daisy Things have been a lot jollier since you twisted your ankle, I admit. Gets us even further away from discovering the Beaumont treasure though. I lie awake at night and think about it.

Trixie No wonder you're looking so pale and ghastly.

Daisy Rot! I'm fit as a fiddle. It would be topping though if we could find it before I leave. I do so want to make it up to everyone for being such a frightful disappointment.

A bell rings off

I must go and join the others on the field.

Trixie Good luck, Daisy, old thing, play up and play the game.

Daisy Thanks awfully, Trixie.

Trixie I saved this doughnut for you, to give you extra strength for the match.

Daisy Trixie, you're a real chum.

Trixie *Hinc spes effulget.*

Daisy exits

Trixie walks over to the window putting aside her crutches

Hinc spes effulget, Daisy, *hinc spes effulget.*

Daisy, Clare, Alice and Belinda enter with hockey sticks. They take up their positions on the pitch. They don't actually move from where they stand

A whistle blows

Bully off. Grangewood have the ball.

Clare Centre forward to right inner.

Alice Right inner to centre forward.

Clare Centre forward to left wing.

Daisy Tackle by Vearncombe!

Trixie Vearncombe have the ball. Don't let them past, oh don't let them past ... they're getting through ... where's the left back ... the left back!

All No.

Trixie Vearncombe have scored the first goal of the match.

A whistle blows for off

Bully-off ... Grangewood again.

Clare Centre forward to right inner.

Alice Right inner to right wing.

Belinda Tackle by Vearncombe!

Trixie Vearncombe take the ball! Left back to left inner ... they're passing down the field. The wing is clear again, mark her! Mark her! Desperate tackle by Clare—to no avail ...

All No!

Trixie Vearncombe score the second goal.

A whistle blows off

Clare Half time.

Clare, Alice, Belinda and Daisy unfreeze from their hockey positions

Belinda Looks as though we shall be beaten hollow.

Daisy Things do look dreadfully grim.

Alice We'll beat them, we must.

Clare I say, chin-up, Grangewood. Vearncombe are a first-rate team but we still have the second half in which to draw level. Those tackles of yours weren't half bad, young Belinda, but you must decide what to do with the ball once you've got it. Daisy, don't let those backs crowd you as they were doing. Remember all of you, when you have the ball, get rid of it fast, don't hug it to yourselves and remember, above all, attack is the best form of defence. We're allowing Vearncombe French leave to do as they wish at the moment. The vantage will be theirs this half with the wind behind them so we must play hard, play up and play the game. Remember—the honour of Grangewood is at stake.

A whistle blows off. Clare, Alice, Belinda and Daisy take their positions again

Trixie They're off.

Clare Centre forward to left inner.

Belinda Left inner back to centre forward.

Clare Centre forward to ...

Trixie Vearncombe snatch the ball. Oh, hard luck!

Daisy Tackle by ...

Trixie Daisy! She's got the ball ... oh quickly, pass it out ...

Daisy Left wing back to right inner ...

Alice Right inner shoots!

All Goal!

Trixie Hurray!

Clare That's the spirit, keep it up.

A whistle blows off

Trixie Vearncombe take the ball! Passing it out to their left wing! Grangewood! Where are you?

Belinda Right half closes in. Drives the ball across to ...

Clare Centre forward to ...

Belinda Right inner. And back to . . .
Clare Centre forward.
Trixie Oh no, Clare's missed it! Don't lose it! Don't lose it! Saved by . . .
Belinda . . . the centre half! A short pass to . . .
Alice Left inner to . . .
Daisy Left wing! Left wing to . . .
Trixie No, Daisy, you're clear! Oh, shoot, Daisy! Shoot! Shoot!
All Goal!
Trixie Two all and seven minutes left to play. Play up school, play up! *Hinc spes effulget*, Daisy! *Hinc spes effulget!* There's some rotten little beasts booing her, led by Sybil no doubt.

The whistle blows for off

Clare Centre forward to right wing!
Alice Right wing to . . .
Trixie Oh, Vearncombe have got the ball! Grangewood! Grangewood! Grangewood!
Clare Tackle by . . .
Trixie Clare! Pass it out! Pass it out! Oh, no! She's gone down on the mud. Jemima! Who's that speeding up the pitch? It's Daisy! She's got the ball!
Daisy Left wing . . .
Belinda To right inner . . .
Alice To centre forward . . .
Clare To left inner . . .
Daisy To left wing . . .
Trixie Shoot Daisy! Shoot! Shoot! Shoot!
All Goal!
Trixie Oh, good shot!

The whistle blows, and there is tumultuous cheering. Everyone hugs each other

Alice Oh, my darlin' girl!
Clare I don't believe it, Alice, we've jolly well won.
Belinda First-rate play, Daisy.
Daisy I did it for Grangewood.
Clare The first time within living memory that anyone has beaten Vearn-combe. Well done all of you, a splendid effort, a game to go down in the annals of Grangewood. But well done to you, kiddie, we've got you to thank for all this. Now off to the Victory tea!

Everyone exits except Daisy and Alice

Alice Are you not coming to the tea, Daisy?
Daisy No, Miss Gibson said I was to go straight back to the San after the match. Don't say anything to Clare, she's so awfully bucked. I wouldn't want to be a wet blanket.

Alice exits

Daisy joins Trixie in the San who has taken up her crutches again

Trixie Capital, Daisy, you were absolutely, uncommonly, spiffingly glorious. Daisy . . .?

Daisy They booed me, Trixie, they booed me.

Trixie exits

Night. A clock chimes twelve. Daisy puts on a dressing-gown and gets into bed

(*Narrating*) Two hours after lights out, try how she might, Daisy could not sleep. The events of the day circled her brain, and the knowledge that largely due to her efforts in winning the hockey-match, the school had been awarded a half-holiday, caused her to ponder even more upon the unworthy actions of those responsible for her present dismal plight. Outside, the wind howled, rattling the window-panes in their frames and sending the waves booming round the headland.

Mr Thompson and Mr Scoblowski enter another part of the stage with a torch which they shine on the ancestral portraits

How queer, someone patrolling the corridors with a torch. Matron is long in bed and surely none of the staff would be up at such an hour, unless the juniors are up to some stunt.

Mr Scoblowski and Mr Thompson exit

"All Through the Night" is heard being whistled

How odd. Perhaps Mr Thompson's planning a burglary . . . what's that?

Winnie Irving enters

I say, Winnie Irving.

Winnie You must come quickly.

Daisy Come? Where to? Whatever's happened?

Winnie Several of us were having a midnight feast in one of the caves in the bay to celebrate today's victory, when suddenly, almost before we had time to notice, the tide crept in covering our path out and so we had to retreat up the side of the cliff. It was only when we reached the top that we realized Monica and Sybil weren't with us. They must have wandered off and also got cut off because we discovered them clinging to a ledge further along the coast. We couldn't find any rope to pull them up with so we thought we'd tie some sheets together to make one. Only thing is, none of us know anything about knots so we thought as you'll probably be expelled anyway and know about knots, we'd enlist your help. Please help us, Daisy. I could wake Miss Gibson, but we'd get into the most fearful row.

Daisy Half a sec. (*She gets out of bed*) You take my sheets (*Narrating*) Daisy and her companion set off along the cliff path that led to the bay.

The Girls act out the story they are telling

Winnie The wind was so strong that it flattened the long grass on the cliff-tops . . .

Daisy And a three-quarters moon scudded in and out of the ragged black clouds.

Winnie Out at sea the wind-whipped waves tossed themselves so high into the air that the two girls could taste the salt-spray on their lips . . .

Dora, Belinda, Sybil and Monica enter

Dora ⎫
Belinda ⎬ *(together)* Winnie!

Winnie We're here.

Daisy Daisy leaned over as far as she dared, and there, many feet below, were the pale, pleading faces of Sybil and Monica. *(To Winnie)* A reef-knot that's what we need. There! That's done! Sybil! Monica! I'm going to throw a line down to you and I want you to grab hold of it and we'll haul you up one at a time.

Winnie Daisy lowered the sheets . . .

Dora A rock tied into the end as ballast . . .

Belinda And presently she felt an answering tug.

Daisy Right-o, heave.

Winnie Slowly but steadily they hauled in the sheet and on the end of it . . .

Sybil Sybil.

Sybil collapses

Daisy Are you all right, Sybil?

Sybil I am . . . but Monica . . . she's in a deadly funk, she won't budge from off the ledge. I tried to persuade her to come up first but she refused point-blank.

Daisy Monica! Monica! It's no good, she's perfectly insensible to anything but her own fear. I'll have to go down and bring her up myself! Now listen you three, I want you to play the line out slowly and then when I'm ready to bring Monica up, I'll give a tug twice on the end of the line and you must pull for all you're worth. Do you understand?

All Yes.

Daisy Right-o, I'm off.

Belinda Gingerly, Daisy swung herself down to the narrow and rapidly crumbling ledge to which Monica clung.

Daisy Monica, I'm going to tie this sheet around your waist to stop you from falling and then I'm going to put my arms round you to make it even less likely that you fall and then we're both going up the side of the cliff together. Understand?

Monica Nooooo!

Daisy Monica if you don't do as I say we'll fall—both of us—into that morass below. Do you understand now?

Monica Yes.

Daisy Good. Daisy tugged twice on the line and slowly Monica began to be hauled up the cliff-face, Daisy frantically searching for hand and foot-holds so as to relieve the burden slightly on the others. We're almost there, Monica, hang on.

Monica Wh ... what's that roaring sound?

Daisy Daisy glanced downwards just in time to see the ledge on which she and Monica had been lately standing disappear into the wild sea. Her heart skipped a beat—just the sea and the wind, Monica, nothing to worry about.

Belinda Practically sweating blood ...

Winnie And almost at their last breath ...

Dora Winnie, Dora and Belinda hauled the now almost unconscious Monica to the top.

Belinda Finally, Daisy herself was pulled to safety.

Dora Whereupon, they all collapsed.

Pause

Belinda I say, we ought to make a move back before we all die of pneumonia.

Daisy Good idea.

Monica I'm dreadfully sorry, Daisy, I was in such a beastly funk.

Daisy I wasn't feeling so tremendously heroic myself.

Sybil Yes, I must say, it was jolly decent of you to rescue us.

Daisy Anyone would have done the same.

Winnie They stumbled along the cliff-path back to school, exhausted in mind and body ...

Daisy Especially Daisy, who after a week of sleepless nights wasn't sure whether or not all that had just happened hadn't been a dream.

Everyone exits except Daisy

Daisy followed last to close the school gates behind the others. She paused, for a final look at the silvery moon illuminating the unruly sea.

Miss Gibson enters

Miss Gibson Daisy Meredith!

Daisy My word! Miss Gibson!

Miss Gibson You were forbidden to leave the Sanatorium without my express permission. Can I place no trust in you? Have you no sense of honour? Well you will flout the rules of Grangewood no longer. See me tomorrow morning in my study at nine. Now go to bed this instant.

Miss Gibson exits

Daisy It's no good, everything I do is wrong, I just don't belong in Grangewood. Perhaps I am as bad as they say I am. But I'm not. I'm not. I can't bear it any longer, I'll run away—that's what I'll do, I'll go back home to mother—and Dick, Douglas, Daniel and Duncan, they love me, they believe in me. Oh, Mother, Mother, I wish, you were here now, I need you so badly ... I'm coming home, Mother, I'm coming home. Hardly conscious of her actions, Daisy passed like a sleep-walker through the school corridors and down into the great hall. Some instinct, she knew not what, caused her to turn and gaze at the grim, commanding portrait of the late Sir Digby Beaumont. Daisy gasped—for the peculiar astronomical device that Sir Digby held was radiating a green glowing light of its own. Luminous paint! Daisy advanced closer to the portrait and there on the rim of the device was depicted a symbol she knew all too well, that of a comet . . .

Mr Thompson enters behind Daisy

. . . the hairy star, and beside it, graven in tiny letters were the words—
"This panel where the hairy star doth shine,
Conceals the treasure, press the symbol mine".

Daisy presses the symbol and the treasure is revealed behind a secret panel

Mr Thompson Daisy.

Daisy turns

Daisy Father. (*She faints*)

There is a Black-out

Everyone enters for Assembly singing "For All the Saints" as the Lights come up

Miss Gibson I have distressing and important news concerning one of your number—Daisy Meredith. At present, Daisy lies dangerously ill in the Sanatorium, suffering, it is suspected, from brain-fever, resulting we think from the trouble in which she has been involved here. She cries wildly in her delirium of dishonour, exams and the like. We fear she may not last the week and she is certainly too ill to be moved to a hospital. However, the crisis point determining whether Daisy lives or dies will be reached this evening and we ask you all to be quieter than usual in your activities, particularly if any of them take place on the lawns outside the San.

Trixie Oh poor, poor Daisy.

Sybil Miss Gibson.

Miss Gibson Yes, Sybil?

Sybil I have something to say which I would like the school to hear as well as you, Miss Gibson.

Miss Gibson Can you not come and tell me later in my . . .

Sybil No, Miss Gibson, I'm sorry, I must speak now.

Miss Gibson Very well, continue.

Sybil Everyone . . . well most people, believe Daisy Meredith to be a cheat, a liar, a sneak and an absolute rotter. Well . . . she isn't. She's one of the pluckiest, most honourable, and sporting girls you could hope to meet. Last night she rescued Monica and me from certain death when we were stranded on a cliff-face after a midnight feast we held, in which she was not involved. It was I who substituted Daisy's name for Trixie's on the winning poem and entered Daisy's poem under my name and came second, I who encouraged another girl in my form to plant the answers to the Geography test in Daisy's book, and I who sneaked on the Second's midnight feast and let Daisy take blame . . . (*She bursts into tears*) I'm a perfectly hateful pig, it's me who should be expelled not Daisy. And if she dies then it's my fault.

Miss Gibson Well, Sybil, I am glad you have had the courage and honour, belated though it is, to confess the true state of things, though I cannot say how sorry I am, that a girl who has been at Grangewood as long as you have, should have fallen into such dark and evil ways. I must ask you to accompany me to my study and to take leave of your class-mates for what I feel will be the last time. It may also interest you to know that the Beaumont treasure has been discovered ...

Everyone gasps

Trixie I say!

Miss Gibson ... by Daisy Meredith and her father who is known to us as Mr Thompson, but whose true identity is that of Sir David Beaumont ...

Clare Uncle David!

Miss Gibson ... the younger son of Sir Digby Beaumont.

Sybil bursts into more tears

Trixie Jemima!

Miss Gibson School dismissed.

Everyone begins to disperse

Trixie O Jubilate! I knew it would all come right in the end, I knew it. (*Narrating*) Daisy's crisis of health that night took its turn ... for the better, and after a day or two, she was able to leave her sick-bed albeit in a weakened condition.

Daisy, her father — Mr Thompson — and Trixie enter the Sanatorium

Mr Thompson You see, my father, Sir Digby Beaumont, objected fiercely to my taking an opera-singer as wife, and after a particularly vehement quarrel with him I left Grangewood for good, changed my name by deed poll, married my sweetheart and moved to Wales.

Daisy Where you had spent many happy boyhood holidays, isn't that right, Father?

Mr Thompson It certainly is, my darling. We bore a family and lived very happily, I earning a living as a doctor until war broke out and so, wishing to serve my country, I enlisted in the Navy. However, one day my ship was torpedoed, sunk and I survived by clinging to a spar of wood in the sea for two days until I was rescued by a passing ship, whereupon I lost consciousness for over a week. On coming to, it was discovered I had lost all memory of who I was and where I had come from — all written proof of my identity having been washed away during my ordeal at sea. I was utterly destitute and friendless and might have remained so, had it not been for a Russian Count on board ship, escaping the horrors of the Revolution, who befriended me. As luck would have it, he was destined for England and after gaining a job at an English Girls' Public School he found work and shelter for me. That teacher's name was ...

Daisy } (*together*) Mr Scoblowski!
Trixie }

Mr Thompson My memory returned gradually over the years and to my surprise, I realized that not only did I work in the grounds of my birthplace but that my daughter was a pupil at the school which had since been founded there. I determined not to reveal myself to Daisy until I could offer her something other than my poverty—though there is no shame in being poor. So, with Mr Scoblowski, I plotted to recover the fortune which my father had hidden.

Daisy That explains Mr Scoblowski's strange manner towards us.

Trixie And also the clue that Sir Digby said lay with his younger son, that tune you were always whistling, Sir David.

Trixie } (*together*) *All Through the Night.*
Daisy }

Mr Thompson Ever my favourite tune, I confess.

Trixie The link with the luminous device . . .

Daisy . . . and the comet . . .

Trixie . . . the hairy star!

Clare enters

Daisy Clare!

Clare Good afternoon, my plucky young cousin. Uncle David. The entire school awaits your return.

Mr Thompson That won't be for a while, I'm afraid, this scholar is going on a convalescing holiday first.

Clare Well deserved, I say.

Trixie Hear, hear.

Clare In a while, if you look out of the window, you will see that wretched imp, Sybil Burlington, depart Grangewood forever.

Daisy They aren't expelling her?

Clare I should jolly well think they are after all that she's confessed to.

Daisy Oh Clare, please don't let them expel her, allow her one last chance. She must have some good in her to have owned up the way she did, it must have taken considerable pluck. It isn't her fault that snobbish attitudes were bred into her, Grangewood can help change them. Please Clare, do be a sport and have a word with Miss Gibson on my behalf.

Clare Very well, child, I'll do my level best, I suppose every worm can turn. I'll catch Sybil before she leaves Miss Gibson's study. But I say, this is all becoming uncommonly dismal. There's to be games and dancing this evening, and the school would simply adore it if you could come down and see them—before you go. Just for a moment. Will you?

Trixie Everyone would be immensely bucked.

Mr Thompson I'll be by your side.

Daisy Very well. It's topping of them to want to see me.

Clare Splendid.

A bell rings off

Trixie Must go, old chum, there's the bell for prep.

Clare Yes, I must go too I'm afraid. I've to supervise the babes. See you later, kiddie.

Clare and Trixie exit

Mr Thompson I'll leave you to dress, Daisy, I must send a telegram to mother.
Daisy Oh father, I'm so tremendously happy.
Mr Thompson So am I, darling, more than I could ever say.

They kiss

Mr Thompson exits

Sybil enters

Daisy Sybil, how absolutely top-hole to see you.
Sybil Daisy . . . you don't know what a beast I've been . . . I'm so . . .
Daisy Sybil, don't.

Daisy and Sybil hug

Sybil You've saved me from expulsion.
Daisy Oh, I'm so frightfully glad you're staying, now we can be friends.
Sybil Can we? Can we really?
Daisy Of course we can, my poor darling. I say, buck-up old thing. Will you come down to the hall with me, I need someone's arm to lean on?

Daisy and Sybil hug

Everyone enters the Great Hall. Some of the girls enter dancing the "Gay Gordons"

Clare Girls, I would like to announce our two guests of honour for this evening, though heaven knows, they need no announcing. First of all, Sir David Beaumont, whom I am very pleased to call Uncle.

Everyone cheers

And secondly, Daisy Meredith or Beaumont, as she will from henceforth be known and whom I am delighted and very proud to call cousin. School—I give you the heroine of Grangewood, Daisy Meredith!

There is very loud cheering

Miss Gibson Quiet, girls, please, Sir David has a few words to say to us all.
Mr Thompson I am not an experienced or indeed a good speaker at the best of times, of which this is one, but I will say that the recovery of the Beaumont treasure has not only enabled me to rediscover my family and disclose my true identity, and keep Grangewood within the Beaumont family, but that some of the money from the treasure will go towards funding a scholarship for another elementary schoolgirl to attend Grangewood which will be called the Daisy Meredith Scholarship.

Everyone cheers

Daisy First of all, thanks awfully for the absolutely top-hole reception you've given my father and me this evening. I'm proud to be once again a girl of Grangewood, of the Upper Fourth.

Belinda We're proud of you, Daisy.

During the course of Daisy's following speech a look of displeasure appears on Miss Gibson's face, which disappears as Clare speaks

Daisy Secondly, I ask you all to accept with open arms the scholarship girls who come to Grangewood. They may have heaps to learn from you about Grangewood's sporting and academic tradition, but my word, have you a lot to learn from them. The beginning we have made here in admitting elementary schoolgirls is small, but I look forward to the day when Grangewood along with other public schools in England, becomes truly public and admits all scholars, monied or not, within its portals of learning and to the day when there is a Grangewood in every city, town and village in England.

There is tumultuous cheering

Clare Girls, girls, before Daisy leaves us for a well-deserved convalesence, I am going to ask her to lead us all in singing the school song. Daisy . . .

The introduction to the school song is played by a teacher on the piano

Trixie Oh Daisy, how perfectly scrummy everything has turned out to be!
Daisy And what fun lies ahead!

School Song

All (*singing*)   In days of yore the female sex
                            Of learning they had none
                            But now thanks to bold pioneers
                            Education they have won.
                            Proud girls and women teach and learn
                            In many a famous hall
                            But of them all there's none more dear
                            Than that of Grangewood School.

                            Long may ye flourish Grangewood School
                            Glorious is thy name
                            Honesta quam magna is our call
                            As we strive to play the game.

CURTAIN

FURNITURE AND PROPERTY LIST

Only essential props and furniture, as mentioned in the text, are listed here. Further dressing should be added at the Producer's discretion

ACT I

Dressing gown **(Daisy)**
School uniform **(Daisy)**
Luggage **(Daisy)**
Package **(Mother)**
Luggage **(Girls and Mistresses)**

Classroom
Desks, seats
Poetry books
Blackboard, chalk and blackboard rubber
Blackboard with writing on it (set for page 00)
Comic
Chalk
Daisy's text book with paper in it

Rubber frog **(Monica)**
Hairbrush **(Sybil)**
Hockey sticks **(Clare and Alice)**
Dressing-gowns **(Sybil and Monica)**
Long black hooded cloaks **(Trixie and Daisy)**
Torch **(Trixie)**
Essay books **(Miss Gibson)**

ACT II

Sock, darning needle **(Daisy)**
Pen and paper **(Trixie)**
Notebook and pencil **(Mr Scoblowski)**
Hockey sticks **(Alice, Clare)**
Bag of buns **(Monica)**
Torch **(Mr Thompson)**
Treasure (set behind secret panel)
Geography book **(Monica)**
Dressing-gown, comic **(Monica)**
Dressing-gown, astronomy book **(Sybil)**
Hot water bottles **(Girls, Daisy, Trixie, Sybil)**
Pencil, paper, pocket dictionary **(Daisy)**
Papers **(Miss Gibson)**
Hockey stick **(Daisy)**
Hockey ball **(Daisy)**
Crutches **(Trixie)**

LIGHTING PLOT

Composite set

Only essential cues, as mentioned in the text, are listed here. Further lighting changes can, and should, be added at the Producer's discretion with regard to staging and facilities available.

ACT I

To open: House Lights up. Stage Lights on (if curtain is raised)

Cue 1	As Miss Gibson and pupils gather on stage *Lower house lights. Increase stage lights*	(Page 1)
Cue 2	Clock strikes two *Night lighting*	(Page 16)
Cue 3	Clare and Alice enter *Daylight*	(Page 17)

ACT II

To open: Darkness

Cue 4	**Voice:** "And two bandy legs." *Lights up to full*	(Page 23)
Cue 5	**Daisy:** ". . . they booed me." *Trixie exits* *Night lighting*	(Page 44)
Cue 6	**Daisy:** "Father." (*She faints*) *Black-Out*	(Page 47)
Cue 7	As Everyone cheers *Lights up to full*	(Page 47)

EFFECTS PLOT

ACT I

Cue 1   **Mother:** "... and you'll pull through."   (Page 3)
Train whistle

Cue 2   **Daisy:** "... I'd been here before."   (Page 7)
Bell rings

Cue 3   **Sybil:** "... or not, all of you."   (Page 11)
Bell rings

Cue 4   **Daisy:** "Hence hope shines forth."   (Page 13)
Bell rings

Cue 5   **Trixie:** "Capital suggestion."   (Page 15)
Bell rings

Cue 6   Sybil and Monica exit   (Page 15)
Clock strikes two

Cue 7   **Trixie:** "How uncommonly rare."   (Page 19)
Bell rings

Cue 8   **Daisy:** *"Hinc spes efflugent."*   (Page 21)
Bell rings

Cue 9   **Daisy:** "... and mountains of Peru."   (Page 22)
Bell rings

ACT II

Cue 10   **Clare:** "... to get complacent, Alice."   (Page 25)
Whistle blows

Cue 11   **Clare:** "... loser. Hip, hip ..."   (Page 28)
Cheering

Cue 12   **Trixie:** "... like the plague."   (Page 32)
Bell rings

Cue 13   Trixie and Daisy exit   (Page 32)
Clock chimes nine

Cue 14   **Trixie:** "... hand in this somewhere."   (Page 39)
Bell rings

Cue 15   **Clare:** "... that's our team."   (Page 39)
Piano music

Cue 16   **Alice:** "... it's a deputy's duty."   (Page 40)
Shrieking and commotion off. Piano playing stops

Cue 17   **Clare:** "... is there good enough?"   (Page 40)
         Piano music

Cue 18   **Daisy:** "... frightful disappointment."   (Page 41)
         Bell rings

Cue 19   Daisy, Clare, Alice and Belinda stand in position   (Page 41)
         Whistle blows

Cue 20   **Trixie:** "... goal of the match."   (Page 41)
         Whistle blows

Cue 21   **Trixie:** "... Vearncombe save the 2nd goal."   (Page 42)
         Whistle blows

Cue 22   **Clare:** "... honour of Grangewood is at stake."   (Page 42)
         Whistle blows

Cue 23   **Clare:** "... keep it up."   (Page 42)
         Whistle blows

Cue 24   **Trixie:** "... led by Sybil, no doubt."   (Page 43)
         Whistle blows

Cue 25   **Trixie:** "Oh, good shot!"   (Page 43)
         Whistle blows. Cheering

Cue 26   As night falls   (Page 44)
         Clock chimes twelve

Cue 27   **Clare:** "Splendid."   (Page 49)
         Bell rings

MADE AND PRINTED IN GREAT BRITAIN BY
LATIMER TREND & COMPANY LTD PLYMOUTH
MADE IN ENGLAND